# Günter Grass

# Literature and Life Series
## Formerly Modern Literature
## (and World Dramatists)

| | |
|---|---|
| Simone de Beauvoir | *Robert Cottrell* |
| Jorge Luis Borges | *George R. McMurray* |
| Albert Camus | *Carol Petersen* |
| Paul Claudel | *Bettina L. Knapp* |
| Colette | *Robert Cottrell* |
| Joan Didion | *Katherine Usher Henderson* |
| T.S. Eliot | *Burton Raffel* |
| E.M. Forster | *Claude J. Summers* |
| Ellen Glasgow | *Marcelle Thiébaux* |
| Christopher Isherwood | *Claude J. Summers* |
| Arthur Koestler | *Mark Levene* |
| Sarah Orne Jewett | *Josephine Donovan* |
| C.S. Lewis | *Margaret Patterson Hannay* |
| André Malraux | *James Robert Hewitt* |
| Mary McCarthy | *Willene Schaefer Hardy* |
| Marianne Moore | *Elizabeth Phillips* |
| Anaïs Nin | *Bettina L. Knapp* |
| José Ortega y Gasset | *Franz Niedermayer* |
| Edgar Allan Poe | *Bettina L. Knapp* |
| Marcel Proust | *James Robert Hewitt* |
| Lionel Trilling | *Edward Joseph Shoben, Jr.* |
| John Updike | *Suzanne Henning Uphaus* |
| Simone Weil | *Dorothy Tuck McFarland* |
| Eudora Welty | *Elizabeth Evans* |
| Oscar Wilde | *Robert Keith Miller* |
| Virginia Woolf | *Manly Johnson* |
| William Butler Yeats | *Anthony Bradley* |
| Emile Zola | *Bettina L. Knapp* |

Complete list of titles in the series available from publisher on request.

# Günter Grass

Richard H. Lawson

Frederick Ungar Publishing Co.
New York

Library of Congress Cataloging in Publication Data

Lawson, Richard H.
    Günter Grass.

        (Literature and life series)
        Bibliography: p.
        Includes index.
        1. Grass, Günter, 1917-        —Criticism and interpreta-
tion.    I. Title.    II. Series.
PT2613.R338Z69    1984        838'.91409        82-40272
ISBN 0-8044-2500-0

Copyright Acknowledgments

"Open Air Concert":
From IN THE EGG AND OTHER POEMS by Günter Grass,
translated by Michael Hamburger, copyright © 1956 by
Hermann Luchterhand Verlag; copyright © 1977 by Günter
Grass. Reprinted by permission of Harcourt Brace Jovanovich,
Inc., and by permission of Martin Secker & Warburg Limited.
Originally published in DIE VORZÜGE DER WIND-
HÜHNER by Hermann Luchterhand Verlag GmbH.

"In the Egg":
From "In the Egg" in SELECTED POEMS by Günter Grass,
translated by Michael Hamburger, copyright © 1960 by
Hermann Luchterhand Verlag GmbH; English translation
copyright © 1966 by Martin Secker & Warburg Limited. Reprinted by permission of Harcourt Brace Jovanovich, Inc., and
by permission of Martin Secker & Warburg Limited. Originally
published in GLEISDREIECK by Hermann Luchterhand Verlag GmbH.

# Contents

# Chronology

| | |
|---|---|
| 1927 | Born on October 16 in Danzig, now Gdańsk, in Poland. |
| 1933-1943 | Attends school in Danzig. |
| 1943 | Leaves school for paramilitary duty in World War II. |
| 1944 | Drafted into the German army. |
| 1945 | Captured by the Americans while recovering from wounds. |
| 1946 | Released from prison camp. |
| 1946-1948 | Works on farm, in a potash mine, and as a stonemason's apprentice. |
| 1948-1951 | Studies at the Düsseldorf Academy of Art. |
| 1952 | Moves to West Berlin to continue studies in sculpture. |
| 1954 | Marries Anna Schwarz. |
| 1956 | Publishes first collection of poems; moves to Paris. |

1959            Publishes *The Tin Drum;* returns to West Berlin.

1961            Publishes *Cat and Mouse;* becomes acquainted with Willy Brandt and begins political involvement.

1963            Publishes *Dog Years.*

1964            Travels to the United States for the first time.

1965            Campaigns for Social Democratic party.

1966            Premiere of *The Plebeians Rehearse the Uprising.*

1969            Premiere of *Max: A Play;* publishes *Local Anaesthetic;* campaigns for Social Democratic party.

1972            Publishes *From the Diary of a Snail.*

1977            Publishes *The Flounder;* collaborates in film production of *The Tin Drum.*

1978            Is divorced from Anna Grass.

1979            Marries Ute Grunert; publishes *The Meeting at Telgte.*

1980            Publishes *Headbirths or The Germans Are Dying Out.*

# Introduction

Günter Grass, born October 16, 1927, comes from a racially mixed, lower middle-class background in the former free city of Danzig (now Polish Gdańsk)—an ancestry and environment that finds extensive direct reflection in his writing. His father's family was German and belonged to the working class: mechanics and carpenters. His father himself owned a grocery store. His mother was of Kashubian origin. (The Kashubians are a Slavic people indigenous to the rural areas around Danzig, quite distinct from the Poles both as to language and culture.) His mother's parents, on migrating to Danzig, became what Grass calls "city Kashubians," spoke German, and aspired to become petty bourgeoisie.

Günter Grass was five years old when the Nazis, having seized power in Germany, began to penetrate the government of the Free City of Danzig. At that time the city was populated almost entirely by Germans but separated from Germany not only politically, under League of Nations stewardship, but also geographically by the surrounding "Polish Corridor" to the Baltic Sea. While a student in the Danzig schools, Grass was a member of the Hitler youth groups corresponding to his age—quite a normal thing in those days. He left school in 1943 to do paramilitary duty. Drafted into the army in 1944, he was wounded in April 1945. At the age of seventeen, while recovering from his wounds, he was captured by the Americans and was a prisoner at the end of hostilities.

Freed in 1946, Grass supported himself for the next two or three years by working on farms, in a potash mine, and as a stonemason's apprentice, until he enrolled as a student of painting and sculpture at the Düsseldorf Academy of Art. A versatile artist, he also played the drum in jazz bands. In 1952 he moved to West Berlin to continue his art studies and subsequently to work as a sculptor and graphic designer. Two years later he married the Swiss ballet dancer, Anna Schwarz, who was to become the mother of his five children.

In addition to his other artistic activity, Grass wrote lyric poetry, in both Düsseldorf and Berlin, some of which he read in 1955 before "Group 47," an influential group of writers dedicated to establishing a new and different German artistic tradition now that the Nazi war was over. To Grass, lyric poetry is the form of art that is the most appealing. In 1955 he joined Group 47 and participated regularly in subsequent annual meetings.

Grass and his wife, now the parents of twin boys, moved to Paris in 1956, where he wrote his first, and immensely successful novel, *The Tin Drum* (1959, 1962). (When two dates are given in this work, the first is that of the German original, the second that of the English translation. Grass's first novel is the only one that had to wait three years before appearing in translation.) Before it was published, he had read portions of it aloud at a meeting of Group 47, which acclaimed his work. In 1960 the Grass family, bolstered by the fame of *The Tin Drum*, again took up residence in West Berlin. By now he had begun writing what shortly emerged as the novella *Cat and Mouse* (1961, 1963) and the novel *Dog Years* (1963, 1965). Together with *The Tin Drum*— deriving from, and reflecting, the people and the ambience of Grass's native city—they comprise The Danzig Trilogy.

Shortly after the appearance of *Cat and Mouse*, Grass was censured by a subministerial official in the state of Hesse for writing obscenities purportedly dangerous to youth. The motion of censure (later withdrawn) was only the tip of the iceberg of prejudice against Grass for his allegedly immoral writings. In any case, the official air may have been cleared a bit by the episode, and Grass continued to write as his artistic integrity demanded. By now, two decades later, the objections of 1962 seem old-fashioned, certainly so when one considers that the objections were European.

After establishing his fame with *The Tin Drum* and *Cat and Mouse,* Grass became active in politics. Perhaps a bit innocently at first, particularly in his outrage at the maligning of Willy Brandt, and then more assertively and with consistent dedication Grass championed the cause of Brandt and the Social Democrats. In his campaign speeches and in his political essays, as in his fiction, Grass inveighs against the prominence and influence of former Nazis in West Germany and against the state of mind in West Germany that preferred the pleasures of conspicuous consumption to the agonizing acceptance of responsibility for Nazi crimes. In Grass's view, Nazism is to be equated with the German lower middle class.

Despite the autobiographical milieu of The Danzig Trilogy, Grass was from the beginning a cosmopolitan writer. We have noted his extended residence in Paris in the late fifties, which was preceded by extensive travel in France and Italy in the early fifties. Since his wife was Swiss, family summers were often spent in the southern part of Switzerland (whose temperate climate, Grass notes, was quite different from the harsh Baltic climate of his own origin). To recreate in his mind the setting of his native Danzig he even had to travel to a foreign country, Poland. By 1960 he had made three trips to Poland. The year 1964 marked the first of several trips to the United States. Other travels included Spain, Israel, England, the Scandinavian countries, Czechoslovakia, Hungary, Romania, Yugoslavia, Greece, the Soviet Union, Italy, Canada, Japan, China, India, Indonesia, Thailand, Hong Kong, and Kenya. His travels— not only the Polish ones—find rather substantial incorporation in his fiction.

Grass's handful of early dramas from the late fifties and early sixties by no means evoked the critical and popular acclaim that his fiction did. In his own view, the basis of all his writing is dialogue. The transition from poetic dialogue to dramatic dialogue, he gives us to understand, was a matter of elaboration and extension; and indeed one can often recognize which poem was extended into which drama. These early dramas, a daring series of pictures far removed from the traditional, may be reckoned in the category of the theater of the absurd, although Grass himself would demur. In 1966, with *The Plebeians Rehearse the Uprising* (English, 1967), bearing on politics, art, and the workers' uprising in Berlin in 1953, he achieved a solid, if not spectacular dramatic success. This was repeated with *Max: A Play* (1969, 1972), in which, while not failing to support reform, he breaks with the radical students of the late sixties, whom, as we can also tell from his essays and interviews, he regards as self-indulgent and whose activities are counterproductive. "Gilded youth" he calls the invaders of a meeting of Group 47, underlining his disdain by using the French phrase *jeunesse dorée,* with its implication of middle-class pampering and indulgence. The characters, plot, and theme of *Max: A Play* are elaborated in the novel *Local Anaesthetic* of the same year. *Local Anaesthetic* was Grass's greatest success in the United States. Grass was featured with it in *Time* magazine, April 13, 1970. The review, while favorable, was, like the biography, somewhat overconcerned in making Grass an apostle of the middle class, an assignment that the facts scarcely sustain.

Grass is emphatically a Socialist. As he describes it himself, he derives his political philosophy from the revisionist, reform, or pragmatic Socialism as advocated in late nineteenth-century Germany: the gradual, step-by-step reform, or evolution, of capitalism into a more equitable system. The student activism of the sixties he opposed because it diverted from the realization of this goal, not because it constituted an annoyance to business as usual.

Consistent with his general political philosophy was Grass's attitude toward the American war in Vietnam as well as toward the Third World, much of which he had seen at first hand. Grass condemned the Vietnam war for what it was. "They do that with napalm," reads a line from a poem; but he did not think that humanity or Socialism or the alleviation of world hunger was served by the excesses of young middle-class protesters in West Germany. Long-range goals are not achieved in the short run, least of all by extraneous violent protest.

As might be expected of a Socialist of Grass's conviction, he is unremittingly opposed to the inhumanity that characterizes the Communist party in the Soviet Union (and East Germany). Stalin and Stalinism are among his favorite metaphors for contemporary wanton, vicious repression. But this doesn't mean at all that he thinks that everything is basically just fine in Western capitalist societies.

Grass's liberal political tenets and his literature are very closely connected—a connection on which he expresses his own views strongly but, over the years, with flexibility. These are expressed in collections of political essays in 1965, 1968, and 1971. He wants to equate morality and politics, at least as closely as possible, and ever more closely. Of course his participation in politics makes him highly vulnerable to criticism. There is but little traditional authority for a German writer of Grass's stature to engage in either hortatory or participatory politics. But according to Grass in 1975, the phrase "literature of engagement" is a tautology—how can literature be other than literature of engagement?; how can a writer be other than an engaged writer?

Grass's political activism reached a peak during the period 1969-1972, when he made numerous political speeches while campaigning for Social Democratic candidates. In the last year of that quite intense and personally demanding activism he published *From the Diary of a Snail* (1972, 1973). It is his ostensible diary as a political campaigner, addressed to his children, above all to his young daughter, interwoven with a fiction based in Nazi Danzig. (The snail is Grass's metaphor for the desirable, because effective, pace of reform.)

The intensity of Grass's political activism seems to have relaxed at least a bit after he began work on the monumental novel *The Flounder* in 1972. The publication of his political essays continued. So did his world travels, including a trip to Israel and New York with his friend Willy Brandt, the Social Democratic political leader and sometime mayor of West Berlin and chancellor of West Germany. The friendship, begun in 1961 when Grass was moved to defend Brandt against the calumnies of his political enemies, continues to the present. It is more a friendship of mutual respect than of uncritical adulation.

Born a Catholic, but anything but a devout believer, and finally an outspoken enemy of the Church, Grass abjured any connection in 1974. He had long seen the Catholic Church as playing an unsavory role in relation to Nazism as well as in the postwar society that in Grass's consistent view retained all too many Nazi vestiges—which could quickly change from being vestiges to harbingers. There is no reason to infer that Grass has any correspondingly greater sympathy with Protestantism.

The German original of *The Flounder* was published in 1977 (English, 1978). In the same year, 1977, Grass participated actively with the film director Volker Schlöndorff in the production of *The Tin Drum* as a movie. He also undertook extensive journeys in Asia and Africa. Although eleven years earlier he had written verse that wittily rejected friends' concerns about the state of his marriage to Anna Schwarz, the Grasses were divorced in 1978. The following year he married the Berlin organist Ute Grunert.

It was also in 1979 that he published the German original of *the meeting at Telgte* (English, 1981). This is a somewhat different kind of historical fiction. Instead of filling out with fiction the interstices in a framework of historical fact, Grass places historical persons, essentially true to their characters, in an extended fictive episode. (Grass is self-taught, but with a formidable range of erudition.) The conjoining of fiction and history, or fiction and autobiography, that characterized *The Flounder* and *The Meeting at Telgte,* also characterizes *Headbirths or The Germans Are Dying Out* (1980, 1982). Grass intervenes—plays a role—in the tale he is narrating. This intervention is related to the leveling of time distinctions, to narrative simultaneity, as well as to a similar leveling of spatial distinction, to equilocation.

Günter Grass's literary reputation seems to be still growing. Despite his involvement—and engagement—in politics, he has consistently refused suggestions that he run for political office. Nonetheless—or perhaps to an extent for that very reason—his political influence is not likely to diminish soon. As matters stand, Grass may well be the best-known living German, and, it would seem, for excellent reasons—for his outstanding literary talent and integrity as well as for his personal and political integrity.

# 1

## The Plays

Grass's early plays, written at about the same time as *The Tin Drum*, failed to obtain critical approval and did not enjoy long runs. Only one of them, *The Wicked Cooks*, was given a Berlin premiere, and that after the sensation caused by *The Tin Drum*. It may be, as Grass suggests, that the German theater was simply not receptive to his innovativeness, that is, his interest in the theater of the absurd—although Grass always kept his distance from the programmatic aspects of absurd theater. It may be that German critics and theatergoers shortly before and after 1960 were conditioned to more traditional drama—even that of Brecht! Still, these early plays, even as they sometimes reflect a perhaps tenuous extension of much more concise poetic origins, have much to offer in the juxtaposition of the serious and the comic, in dramatic adroitness, in clever situations and lines, and in posing questions to which there are no easy answers (perhaps no answers at all). Further, they provide a good insight into the preoccupations and even the methods of Grass, the world-renowned novelist.

The highly experimental curtain raiser, *Rocking Back and Forth,* was produced in 1958. The "back and forth" of the title may lead us to anticipate an ambivalence of direction, and this is in fact what the play—or is it just an onstage discussion?—is about. The dramatic action of *Rocking Back and Forth* is not action, but words that theorize about dramatic action and thus inhibit or prevent action.

An anachronistic circus clown, Conelli, rocks back and forth on a rocking horse as he discourses about drama with a Director, an Actor, and a Playwright. This less than unified triumvirate rack their brains to find a way to incorporate the Clown covertly into the theater, but he remains true to his own, vanishing art. He is not tempted down from his rocking horse, which he calls Ingeborg, not even by a bed hauled onto the scene supposedly containing the Actor's wife. Conelli, seeing no need to introduce dramatic conflict, suggests alternatively that if, as it appears, the invented wife is pretending to be a dead rabbit because she is being kept waiting, then it would be best if all three pretended to be dead rabbits. (Here Grass, a master of creative punning, is undercutting the Clown's undercutting by punning on his name, Conelli: compare Italian *coniglio* "rabbit," or even the first, root syllable of German *Kaninchen.)*

A piano and its black-and-white animal counterpart, zebras—the same object-animal conjoining as in an early Grass poem, "Prevention of Cruelty to Animals"—likewise fail to enlist the Clown's participation in action. He simply will not leave his rocking horse. "The conflict is long overdue!" remarks the Director, all too tellingly. Finally the Clown consents to get into bed with the Actor's imaginary wife, but only if the rocking horse, Ingeborg, is permitted to join them. Once in bed, the Clown denies dramatic conflict definitively by playing dead—and apparently expecting Ingeborg to do the same!

Thus Grass's play rocks back and forth between discourse and dramatic realization (or nonrealization). What tension

there is comes across as more intellectual, or perhaps only
more clever, than dramatic. In the process Grass seems even
to question the underlying agonistic or argumentative idea of
drama. Any dramatic possibilities, such as the marriage of
Conelli's daughter to a film-splicer, are arbitrarily precluded
by Conelli's manner of adamantly opposing the match and
meanly diminishing the film-splicer, and even more
devastatingly by Grass's manner of allowing the film-splicer
to be made a buffoon—by a Clown! It seems that no drama
is possible. In the end the Clown is back on his rocking
horse, rocking back and forth, and nothing has changed.

The subtitle of *Rocking Back and Forth* is *Prologue on
the Stage*. The original German, *Vorspiel auf dem Theater*,
cannot fail to evoke in the German playgoer or reader the
identical title of the prologue to Goethe's *Faust*. In the *Faust*
prologue Goethe brings together the Director, the Poet, and
the Comedian to discuss the nature and techniques of
dramatic production. Their earthy and perceptive discussion
is concluded with a call to action, at which the drama proper
commences. But Grass's inventive and witty parody of
Goethe's prologue never results in dramatic action; indeed
quite the opposite. The very theme of the play may well be
its chief shortcoming as drama.

Grass's first produced play of longer than curtain-raiser
length was *Flood*, which had its premiere in January 1957.
Like all the early dramas, it was written at the time Grass was
working on *The Tin Drum*. And like most of the coeval
dramas it is quite clearly an elaboration of an early poem, also
called "Flood." Here again we have the negation of a
dramatic situation. As the rains pour and the floodwaters rise
relentlessly in his house, the owner Noah—his name is one of
the most transparent examples of Grass's often ironically
significant nomenclature—is struggling to move his collection
of historic inkwells and candelabra up from his basement.
His sister-in-law Betty worries more about saving photograph
albums, her pickled mementos of the past. In the room
above are Noah's daughter Yetta and her insecure boyfriend

Henry. (Where proper names in the English translation differ from those in the original German, I use the English forms.) Yetta and Henry are painful caricatures of modern youth, predictably concerned with preserving their phonograph records, magazines, and beer, but otherwise evincing little concern about the impending catastrophe. They are too bored to help Noah and, evidently depressed if not worried by the rain, even too bored to have sex. Finally, on the roof of the threatened house sit two large, articulate, and quite sensible rat masks, Pearl and Point.

There now arrive from distant travels, stepping out of a crate—Grass has a liking for direct stage entrances of this kind—Leo, Noah's son, and Congo, Leo's friend, said to be a former boxer. The partly incorporeal love triangle in *Rocking Back and Forth* is here fleshed out: Henry, hardly resisting, is put out on the roof, while Yetta hops into bed with the sensual Congo, for "as long as it rains," singing a song to elaborate her point. Aunt Betty sews parasols against the inevitable day when the rain stops and the sun shines. Noah sorts his inkwells. Henry endures resignedly his banishment from Yetta's favors, already prepared to forgive her. From their particular point of view Pearl and Point comment on the goings-on.

The rains abate, the flood gradually disappears. But no one is elated. In Leo's words, after the rain comes "the beginning of the Ice Age." Perhaps the excitement, the dramatic possibility inherent in the flood was better after all. As they planned, Leo and Congo depart for the North Pole (or maybe Liverpool). For their part, Pearl and Point, expecting the return to normalcy to signal the return of rat traps, prepare to depart for Hamelin. Yetta and Henry are glumly reconciled.

As in the early poems, in *Flood* Grass puts his people, animals, and things (the inkwells, the candelabra, the crate out of which Leo and Congo leap) into unusual relationships with each other. In *Flood* it is the rising water that forces the unusual juxtapositions. But as in *Rocking Back and Forth* the only possible dramatic movement is thwarted: when the rain ends, everything goes back to normal. The clever but often abstract discussion that accompanies this absence of dramatic movement probably contributed to the failure of *Flood* to gain popular or critical success. In 1957, after all, German drama had enjoyed a centuries-long, essentially uninterrupted tradition of didacticism, quite at odds with the absurd theater of *Rocking Back and Forth* and *Flood*.

*Mister, Mister,* a play in four acts, was premiered in 1958. The central figure, who ties the play together by appearing in all four acts, as well as in the prologue of each act, is a "systematizer" named Bollin. In addition to his structural function of systematizing the play itself, Bollin is, or would like to be, an enforcer of his own ideas of order, through the means of murder. His intended victims, however, do not take the pedantic would-be murderer very seriously, nor do events proceed as his too logical mind had anticipated, and in the end he is himself slain.

The prologue to the first act introduces Bollin sitting on a park bench. He offers candy to two teen-age children skating around him, the thirteen-year-old girl, Sprat, and the fourteen-year-old boy, Slick. The children decline the candy but tease him for a more substantial handout:

Mister, mister, aintcha got a thing,
Mister, just a little thing,
Any little thing.
Mister, mister, aintcha, aintcha,
Aintcha, aintcha, aintcha got
Any little dingus,
Hidden in your pocket?

Bollin shakes his fist at them and their refrain, with its vague allusion to sex and to concealed weaponry. As he leaves he threatens: "If they don't want candy, they'll get something else."

Indeed, the "thing" turns out to be Bollin's revolver, when we get to the main part of act 1, as well as his sexual designs on the sixteen-year-old Sophie. Sophie is in bed with the flu, but despite her fever she reacts with indifference to Bollin's emergence from under her bed, to his threats both murderous and lecherous, and to his pedantic penchant for assembling statistics. She chats with him, warns him to keep his distance owing to the possibility of infection, and solicits his help in completing her crossword puzzle. The futility of Bollin's mission with Sophie is ludicrously reinforced by the appearance of Sophie's mother, a widow who does not long delay making advances to him. Thwarted, Bollin pockets his revolver, steals Sophie's doll named Pinky, and departs. In the prologue to act 2 he takes out his frustrations on Pinky in two ways; sexually, by thrusting a knife into the doll's belly, then sewing up the rent and suggesting to himself that twice a week is enough; murderously, by hanging the doll up on a hook and after missing three frontal shots shooting it in the back.

The main part of act 2 finds Bollin in the woods. He digs and covers a pitfall, into which his intended victim, the forester, wanders while following Bollin's cuckoo calls. The forester proves as fearless and inappropriate a victim as Sophie, diverting Bollin's intentions with a botany lecture, including a version for Sprat and Slick, who show up in the woods picking blueberries. In the prologue to act 3 Bollin takes out his frustration by chopping down a Christmas tree.

In act 3 proper, Bollin, crashing through a dressing screen, finds his third intended murder victim, the opera singer Mimi Landella, in her bathtub during a photo session. But her irrepressible chatter diverts him from his purpose. A duet with Mimi finds him mouthing but not singing words from *The Barber of Seville*. When the soprano makes advances—having already changed his name from Bollin to Pollino, which is Spanish for "ass" or "fool"—Bollin shakes loose, insisting emphatically that "Bollin is and remains normal."

Bollin has aged and become rather seedy in act 4. Alone at an abandoned building on the outskirts of the city, he is joined once more by Sprat and Slick. Again they taunt him with the allusive chant of "Mister, mister." They gradually persuade him to let them inspect his watch, his pen, and his revolver, all of which they keep, for Bollin is lame and cannot run after the children. Sprat, playing with the revolver—the "thing"—accidentally shoots Bollin dead. As for the corollary significance of "thing," Sprat and Slick, hardly contrite about the killing, head for a barn for teen-age sexual experimentation, half singing the title refrain as they go.

The thing as revolver—as an object—has proved superior to people, not only in repeatedly frustrating Bollin's intentions, but also, finally, in serving as the means of his death. In a sense the thing as sexual totem—as an object—likewise dominates people like Sprat and Slick. To judge from their sexual misinformation, they have not dallied seriously before coming into possession of the revolver.

Bollin himself may be seen in at least two aspects of character, neither of which necessarily excludes the other. In his harmless pedantry, his continual flubbing, his final defenselessness against the teasing and the thievery of Sprat and Slick, finally in his shocking and unmourned death, he may well enlist our sympathy and grief. We will have been persuaded to forget that he is a professional killer and apparently a practiced molester of young girls as well.

There is more, although it is inferential, based in part at least on our knowledge that the playwright of *Mister, Mister* was at the same time the writer of *The Tin Drum*, a scathing indictment of the crimes of Nazism. In his coexistent pedantry and brutality, Bollin is not unlike a composite of Nazi middle-level administrators. That is true especially in his continually waiting for word from his "uncle Max" before he can act; and in his violent insistence: "Bollin is and remains normal! . . . Bollin is normal!" A more convincing, more specific detail, links Bollin with Nazism in the way he "executes" the doll Pinky: "He stands up, pulls down a hook suspended from the ceiling, and hangs the doll on it." Hooks suspended from ceilings are perhaps most commonly found in slaughterhouses. It is notorious that the Nazis used a slaughterhouse attached to Plötzensee Prison in Berlin to execute members of the generals' conspiracy, stringing the condemned up on carcass hooks suspended from the ceiling before hanging them. Altogether some two thousand political prisoners were executed at Plötzensee, to which Grass refers specifically in a political drama, *Max: A Play.*

The one-acter *Only Ten Minutes to Buffalo* was first presented in 1959. Although the action takes place on a Bavarian meadow, the Buffalo in the ironic title is indeed Buffalo, N.Y. Or at least it is the metaphor of Buffalo, N.Y., as a goal after travail and trial, such as it is in the American ballad of "John Maynard," a Lake Erie helmsman who refused to desert his fire-ravaged ship. In Grass's play, whose two principal characters are translated from an essay he was writing at the same time, "Content as Resistance," we have the locomotive engineer Krudewil and his fireman Pempelfort driving in their fantasy a rusty and moss-grown locomotive across the green landscape, with cows in the background and the painter Kotschenreuter in the foreground. The latter, who is in fact painting a seascape, explains to Axel the cowherd, one has only to use one's imagination; everything, cow, ship, painter, and buttercup are only names, hallucinations.

While Krudewil and Pempelfort fantasize, "in thirty minutes we'll be in Buffalo," and Kotschenreuter falls victim to his own conceptualizing, the naive Axel has been spurred to perception. He finds it possible to exploit the tension, the enmity of form and content (a favorite idea of Grass) and to unite imagination and reality. In the latter part of the play Grass adds the grotesque figure of Frigate, a female admiral with a frigate for a hat, who barks nautical commands to her conscripted, landlocked crew. Finally, the principal object, the locomotive, actually begins to roll, at which moment the play ends.

Amidst the confusion and the clever repartee, two themes stand out in *Only Ten Minutes to Buffalo*. First is the theme revolving about Axel—possibly Grass's alter ego—the free artist who violates the rules of art to produce art while others only theorize or fall victim to conceptualization. Second is the theme revolving about the locomotive, a possible metaphor of the drama of the absurd, fired by fantasy but retarded by artistic debate, heading toward an unreachable goal.

*Only Ten Minutes to Buffalo,* containing a dramatic situation (not as in *Flood* the negation of a dramatic situation) as well as a bit of genuine dramatic action, may well be Grass's most effective work for the theater; certainly it is, among his early plays. In a sense Grass as free artist here escapes the trap of conceptualizing even as his character Axel accomplishes the same feat. As in his other early plays the repartee is so ready at hand, so clever, that one is tempted to judge it as too clever by half. But in *Only Ten Minutes to Buffalo* the repartee seems less susceptible to categorization as a substitute for a developed dramatic situation.

Grass's personal interest in gastronomy and cooking is paralleled by frequent artistic use of themes related to cooking. One early example is the poem "Chefs and Spoons." The concise poem prefigures the elaborate five-act play, *The Wicked Cooks,* which had its premiere in 1961. By that time Grass was a celebrated novelist, but his fame was still not up to rescuing *The Wicked Cooks* from a tepid reception. Clever as it is, as theater its effect is weakened by overextension of what is a fairly slight premise, generously supplemented by pantomime, stage business, and dance.

Five cooks, Petri, Grün, Vasco, Stach, and Benny are trying to wheedle the recipe for a marvelously successful soup from one Herbert Schymanski, called "the Count." An amateur cook, Schymanski concocted the soup some while ago for a restaurateur and is not disposed to give out his recipe. The cooks materialize in characteristic Grass fashion: from the bell of a trumpet, from a huge egg, from a stove.

Antic cooks, they dance, they sing, they play about like children. In act 1 Vasco, accosting the Count on a bridge, attempts to force the recipe from him, losing his own hat over the bridge in the vain struggle. The Count merely notes that it is "a very ordinary cabbage soup" with "a very precise amount of very special ashes." Martha, a nurse, Vasco's fiancée, who is on her way to attend Vasco's critically ill aunt, is briefly introduced in the same scene.

Act 2 takes place at the apartment of Aunt Therese, who is now attended by both Vasco and Martha. The former, grilled by his aunt, claims to have been in church and to have prayed—although one may well doubt it. The act ends with the several cooks singing and dancing. In act 3 the restaurateur Schuster announces impending bankruptcy unless the cooks can contrive to get the recipe for the marvelous soup. Again the Count refuses to cooperate. Not until act 4 do the cooks realize that in their quest they have an ace in the hole: Vasco's fiancée Martha, to whom the Count is attracted. After repelling a gang of rival cooks crashing a party, the cooks persuade Vasco to agree to the proposed romantic match of Martha and the Count—in effect the recipe for love in exchange for the recipe for soup. Somewhat confused, but willing to play the game, Martha too, agrees.

Martha marries the Count. Some time elapses before the events of act 5, which are not the anticipated events at all. The marriage turns out to be a true love match. In fact, so in love with Martha is the Count that he has quite forgotten the soup recipe: "The last few months with Martha, with my wife. . . . It has made this experience [= the recipe ] superfluous. I have forgotten it." And in any case it is not really a set recipe at all, but, as the Count says, "an experience . . . continuous change." (Those concepts, those phrases are unalloyed Günter Grass, the emergent Socialist reformer.) But the cooks keep pressing. Since the Count and Martha cannot comply with the original bargain, they commit suicide. The cooks scatter.

*The Wicked Cooks* is probably too long for the simple motif on which it is based—the futile quest of the recipe. The diffuseness of the action, the singing, the dancing, the stage business such as feigning tennis with frying pans, do not compensate for the long periods of absence of dramatic movement. On the other hand, or perhaps just because of the uncertainty of focus and the absence of movement, the play seems to be particularly rich in interpretive possibilities. The nomenclature already suggests the Bible and church history: Benny (Benjamin), Stach (Eustachius), Martha, Petri, and Therese, for example. The nicknames among the standard names suggest no great respect for Bible or church. The potential saviour, the Count with an apparently Polish-Jewish name, Schymanski, strikes Christ-like attitudes, and even his death is not without blasphemous resonance. The difficulty with all of this and with other half-parallels is that they apply only to a limited portion of the total play. (It might be said that the diffuseness of the play ultimately defeats its own compensation by way of interpretation.)

In the first production of *The Wicked Cooks*, the actor playing the Count wore a mask made to look like Günter Grass. However much a prank that may have been, it at least suggests the possibility of considering *The Wicked Cooks*, like *Rocking Back and Forth*, as a parable on the dilemma of the artist. Shall the Count, the artist, the aristocrat of the mind, yield to the mass conformity of the cooks in their indistinguishable white uniforms? Or shall he preserve his individuality, his artistic integrity?

A political interpretation, which like the others focuses on the amenable facets at the expense of the total play, would extend the cooks' indistinguishability and conformity to that of adherents of a totalitarian state, such as the Nazi state. The recipe, which does not exist in the present, would be that of the perfect society. And the cooks, while plying an innocent and even jolly trade, are in fact inhumane, even brutish (for example, in the manipulation of Martha). If the white uniforms pose a problem for this line of interpretation, they may be seen as reverse code for black uniforms. But clearly the entire play cannot be made subject to such ad hoc reductionism.

Again, *The Wicked Cooks* may to an extent be regarded as a drama of the absurd, although implicit in that assertion is the recantation of the artistic explanation of the Count's suicide. Were *The Wicked Cooks* a true absurd drama, we would have to regard the Count's death as pointless (which, in a sense, it is, no matter what its impetus). Also pointing in the direction of the absurd is the long waiting in vain for a solution, the long stretches that lack dramatic movement, retarded by farcical interludes. It is certainly preferable not to insist on the absurd or on any single line of interpretation, because any single exclusive interpretation subtracts from the fundamental ambiguity of the play. It is little wonder that Grass has scant patience with interpretations of his works.

Representative of the general critical estimate that Grass's early plays are thin from the point of view of theater, Marianne Kesting would prefer that the five acts of *The Wicked Cooks* be condensed into one act.[1] Grass's early plays, whose chief dramatic effect is their imagistic quality—most trenchantly developed in *Only Ten Minutes to Buffalo*—on that account do not perhaps hold up well as theater when the playwright extends them to two or more acts. In the resultant tension, which is anything but dramatic tension, it is not difficult to see the underlying source of the antagonism between Grass and the *Dramaturgen,* or play-adapters, whose business it is to shape the play for the German theater.

The dramas considered thus far, all written during the period 1954-1957 (despite later dates of publication and premieres), can be brought together in a category that Grass himself actually calls "absurd theater" and "poetic theater." If he is a trifle ironic in offering the latter term (not to mention the former), it has nonetheless been picked up by critics and become part of the critical vocabulary; moreover, the term has the virtue of reminding us that most of the dramas from 1954-1957 were in fact dramatic elaborations of poems. In Grass's later dramatic phase, represented chiefly by *The Plebeians Rehearse the Uprising* and *Max: A Play* (sometimes called *Uptight*), he writes what can be called "dramas of retardation." Here the dramatic conflict, elusive or absent in the drama of the absurd, exists between action and retardation of action, between doing and not doing, between action and words (although the words may be *about* action). Thematically, in the ultimate absence or abortion of action, this type of drama is perhaps not such a far step from the absurd as some critics (and Grass himself) urge; it is, however, discernible as structurally different.

In the way that Bertolt Brecht is perceived by Grass to have proceeded from epic theater to dialectic theater, Grass sees himself as moving from absurd, poetic theater to dialectic theater as well. In the latter, plot does not unreel; rather, the drama proceeds from thesis to antithesis to synthesis, even as, in *The Plebeians,* the classical unities of time, place, and action are quite strictly observed. If for "antithesis" one reads "retardation," with the dramatic tension that it is bound to create, one is taking a probably comfortable step from theory into practice.

*The Plebeians Rehearse the Uprising: A German Tragedy* was first performed in West Berlin in 1966, with moderate success. The American premiere was of a seriously emasculated version by the Harvard Dramatic Club in 1967. In England, the full version, with minor changes in staging (Grass's characteristic retardation of action tends unfortunately to leave actors hanging around on stage not doing much) was presented in 1970 with great success by the Royal Shakespeare Company.

The scene of *The Plebeians* is Berlin, East Berlin, eight years before the Communists erected the Wall to keep their people from leaving. That makes the date 1953. More precisely it is June 17, 1953, the date of the failed workers' uprising against the increased work norm—a "stretch-out" in American labor terminology—imposed for the first time unilaterally by the Communist bureaucracy without the customary charade of the workers initiating a stretch-out on their own. Grass is careful to avoid calling the uprising a revolution, which it wasn't. The more precise scene is the Berlin theater of "The Boss." Grass has given The Boss numerous, quite easily identifiable characteristics of Bert Brecht. Brecht, as is well known, significantly failed—along with all the East German intelligentsia, not to speak of the Western—to give aid, direction, or support to the leaderless and confused uprising of the workers, which, within a few hours' time changing from reformist ("let us return to bearable norms") to political ("let us have a free election"), was ruthlessly put down by Soviet tanks. But *The Plebeians* is not an anti-Brecht polemic, not a denunciation of Brecht's poor courage but sound judgment (the uprising failed). Grass uses the figure of Brecht not as a personality, but first, as a model or representative of all the "chicken-hearted radicals" in both East and West Germany who failed to act on June 17, 1953, and second, more importantly, as a model of the dilemma of the artist who tries to balance his political attitudes with his artistic commitment. For Brecht, the professional aesthete in a totalitarian state, the dilemma is especially severe.

Whereas the real Brecht was rehearsing a different play on June 17, Grass has The Boss rehearsing *Coriolan,* Brecht's adaptation of Shakespeare's *Coriolanus.* In the latter, the plebeians are unworthy and in any case play no key role; Coriolanus, as the enemy of the plebeians, is not thereby a friend of the patricians; the tragedy ends with his fall. Brecht's Coriolan, reduced from Shakespeare's encompassing figure to a mere military specialist, is a friend of the patricians; Brecht's plebeians are idealized, and the play ends with their triumph.

Midway in the first act of *The Plebeians,* in which The Boss's *Coriolan* is being rehearsed in The Boss's theater, the rehearsal is interrupted by an incursion of workers onto the rehearsal stage. They have come from the uprising in the street, a picture of The Boss in hand so that they can recognize him. Their mission is to get from The Boss a written statement of support for the uprising. The Boss, whose revolutionary credentials go back at least to the turbulent 1920s, demurs. Now the compleat aesthete, to whom a perfect presentation of Marxist drama is more important than the lending of support to a workers' uprising, he fends and fences dialectically and didactically with the simple workers. He knows the fruits of failed uprising—even failed revolution—all too well and he knows the nature and habits of his petitioners all too well. He wavers and stalls on making a commitment, even as a succession of reports on the uprising are brought in from the street.

The Boss's role as an artist, and as an artist in the service of the Communist state—there has been talk of providing a revolving stage for his theater—comes into conflict with his formerly lively but now evidently atrophied revolutionary enthusiasm, and the artist wins. There is moreover an artistic bonus in the continuing confrontation with a series of workers; the opportunity to record their speeches on tape as a means of increasing the verisimilitude of his plays portraying workers. Thus Grass underscores, with mild irony, The Boss's essential commitment to art. But artistic commitment not without a struggle, not without flashes of possible commitment to action, only in turn to be retarded by new incident—or rather report of new incident.

News of the progress, the absence of progress, the heroics, and the failure of the uprising is brought to the theater by new groups of workers. As these reports impinge on The Boss's struggle, perhaps tempting him to commitment, more often dissuading him from commitment, his potential for action is subject to repeated retardation. The first workers, who desire only a small improvement as a first step in reform—who are thus in tune with Grass's own idea of reform—are supplemented by already politicized workers who demand instant action. In their frustration, the politicized workers even string up The Boss and his dramatic adviser for hanging, only to be deterred in turn by the latter's recitation of the somewhat obscene Shakespeare parable of the belly and the rest of the body, in which for present purposes the belly represents the state, the central and supporting organ for everything else. Like The Boss, the adviser knows his proletarians: they are delighted by the gross aspects of the tale and do not question the belly-state analogy. The nooses are removed from the necks of The Boss and his colleague.

In contrast to The Boss's tortuous line of response to the incidence of retardation—which may be thought of as comprising antithesis—is the straight line of modification in the responses of Volumnia. So called from her role in *Coriolan*, she is The Boss's closest associate, both personally and professionally, his wife, his intimate, his colleague. To the extent that The Boss is a model of Brecht and all the radical intellectuals who failed the uprising, Volumnia then is the model of Helene Weigel, Brecht's wife. As Volumnia counsels The Boss, her counsel runs the gamut from the bathos of lyrical revolutionism to, finally, expeditious self-interest and flight.

Ironically, owing to the lag in reports of events on the street, The Boss is on the verge of supporting the uprising after the Soviet tanks and machine guns have quelled it. "Don't pretend to be blind," advises Volumnia, showing The Boss a leaflet signed by the Soviet commandant, which is the final retardant. The antithesis is complete. The Boss's synthesis, hinted at previously by Grass's masterful incorporation of allusive lyric motifs from Brecht, is to abandon his *Coriolan* and go to the country. It is rather sad. It is also inconsonant with the notion that *The Plebeians* is an anti-Brecht polemic.

To some extent that incorrect assertion springs from the incorrect assumption that *The Plebeians* is a documentary drama, an emergent genre in the mid-1960s, and thus that The Boss and the circumstances depicted are to be understood as direct reflections of historical reality. And it is inevitably true that in selecting a dramatic topic so nearly contemporary as Brecht and the workers' uprising, Grass impales himself on the dilemma of how, how much, and where to exercise the artist's prerogative of modifying events hardly shaded by the passage of time. However the problem is solved, the solution guarantees misapprehension. But on an even more objectifiable level, by no means devoid of political implications, it is Grass who bears the ultimate responsibility for the misapprehension that *The Plebeians* is anti-Brecht.

In 1964, before he began writing *The Plebeians,* Grass delivered an address at the Berlin Academy of Arts and Sciences. The title reflects his erudition, his not at all bashful self-estimate, and probably a little self-irony as well: "The Prehistory and Posthistory of the Tragedy of Coriolanus from Livy and Plutarch via Shakespeare down to Brecht and Myself." In a brilliant but methodologically almost old-fashioned display of literary-historical scholarship, Grass charges Brecht with falsifying Shakespeare, with manipulating his borrowed material to serve an ideological purpose. Thus Grass in a sense *was* anti-Brecht in the address of 1964.[2] But he was not—or certainly to a far lesser extent—in the drama of 1966. Two years of wrestling with the concept of the complex Boss, with the artist's dilemma vis-à-vis politics—even as Grass's own involvement in politics deepened—had made Grass a more sympathetic playwright in 1966 than he was a speaker in 1964.

**2**

## *The Tin Drum*

There is some suggestion that Grass, piqued at his extremely modest success, or actually *lack* of success with his early dramas, set to work on *The Tin Drum* in something of an "I'll show them" spirit. If so, he surely succeeded beyond his most sanguine expectations. The dubiously successful dramatist, the poet whose verse, however meritorious, had failed to find much public acceptance, became a hugely successful novelist with *The Tin Drum*. Public acceptance of the novel when it appeared was decidedly not unanimous. In the fifties and early sixties charges of blasphemy and pornography could still be sustained, at least in the short run. By 1965 such carping, both legal and critical, had largely subsided, and the novel was on its way to becoming a classic of post-World War II literature, an international as well as a German classic.

Success in this case begets success. Grass, anything but a novelistic flash in the pan, has continued to write prose of the standard set by *The Tin Drum*, even though not necessarily (after The Danzig Trilogy, of which *The Tin Drum* is the

19

first part) on a par with *The Tin Drum*. It is reasonable to suppose too that the movie of the same name, premiered May 4, 1979, directed by Volker Schlöndorff in close association with Günter Grass, has contributed to the continuing success and reception of the novel.

As Grass declares, he aimed with *The Tin Drum* to break away from the prose fashion of the fifties, which in the wake of Franz Kafka was continuing to offer up "timeless and placeless parables. . . . I bypass parables, and I have a direct connection with geography and with time."[1] Expressed in somewhat different terms, Grass is restating for his novel the fundamentality of objects, the same fundamentality that hitherto had prevailed in his poetry and his plays. The fundamental object in *The Tin Drum* is Nazism. We see it in all its evocations, in all its crimes, but we are never far from the sense that it is at bottom a political movement, sprung from and enlisting the German lower middle class—Oskar Matzerath's people.

The primary geographic setting of the novel is Günter Grass's native city of Danzig, formerly in German West Prussia, now the Polish port of Gdańsk. With Danzig, both in *The Tin Drum* and in much of his subsequent fiction, Grass retains a direct, sometimes poignant connection. In book 3 of the novel, after Oskar's flight at the end of World War II, the setting is Düsseldorf, West Germany. The times in *The Tin Drum* are the periods 1952 to 1954 and 1899 to 1954. While we are encouraged to see a cyclicity or identity of events during those two periods, the periods themselves are clearly demarcated. In other words, despite cyclicity or similarity of events time itself in the novel is not circular. It proceeds in a straight line, conservatively and chronologically, not much more complicatedly, if only one keeps the two levels and periods in mind, than in a novel of the nineteenth century. The complexities of *The Tin Drum* are of a different order.

During the period 1952-1954 the twenty-eight to thirty-year-old Oskar Matzerath writes his memoirs as an inmate of an insane asylum. To be sure, Oskar discourses with at least seeming rationality about his writing project—his auto-biographical novel. It is not to be a modern novel that dispenses entirely with time and place, or even one that begins in the middle of things. Nor is it to be a novel lacking, in the modern fashion, a hero. It will have two heroes, says Oskar: Oskar himself, who is inside a door equipped with a peephole, and Bruno Münsterberg, his keeper, who watches him through the peephole (and has obtained the paper on which Oskar writes). At the moment Oskar seems to be involved in some kind of litigation, for among his not very welcome once-a-week visitors is his lawyer.

Oskar, continuing in a literary-critical vein, feels that any autobiography is an impertinence unless the author has the patience "to say a word or two about at least half of his grandparents before plunging into his own existence." (The concept "plunge" will turn out to be a highly important one for Oskar.) He introduces us to his grandmother Anna in 1899 and thus to the longer time period of the novel, which like the shorter period will end in 1954. Toward the end the two periods converge or overlap. The end point of both is Oskar's thirtieth birthday in September 1954.

We meet Anna Bronski—Anna Koljaiczek as a young woman before her marriage—in a potato field in Kashubia sitting before a fire trying to keep warm. She is wearing four skirts, a protection that serves as a motif on which Oskar dwells lovingly in connection with his grandmother, for later these voluminous skirts became his frequent childhood refuge from an altogether distasteful world. At the present moment they are also a refuge for the arsonist Joseph Koljaiczek in his flight across the potato fields ahead of two not very bright policemen. While hiding under Anna's skirts, Joseph begets Oskar's mother—"my poor mother," Agnes Koljaiczek.

Joseph Koljaiczek is an arsonist in an era when setting fire to sawmills in the area around Danzig—that is, West Prussia under German rule—was a symbol of Polish patriotism. But

Joseph Koljaiczek's career as a firebug ends while his daughter Agnes is still a nursing infant. Fleeing the gendarmes again he jumps from float to float, from log to log, on a pond in the Mottlau River. His pursuers fire at him, he jumps from the last float into the water and disappears under the logs. Some say he drowned, although others are less certain. There are even stories that he got to Buffalo, N.Y., and became a millionaire as a stockholder in match companies and as a founder of several fire insurance companies.

As Oskar's future mother Agnes grows up, she falls in love at seventeen with her cousin Jan Bronski, a frail young man turned down four times for military service in World War I. Their relationship had been more than cousinly for some time, Oskar believes, and yet Anna Koljaiczek apparently put up with it. But Agnes does not marry Jan. She falls in love with a wounded soldier in the hospital where she is serving as an auxiliary nurse. Alfred Matzerath, from the Rhineland, captivates all the nurses with his merry ways—especially Agnes, who appreciates additionally his talent for cookery.

Alfred Matzerath remains in Danzig after World War I, representing the paper firm for which he had previously worked in the Rhineland. Later, after marrying Agnes, he becomes a business partner with her in successfully running a grocery store. Jan Bronski, the stamp collector with his roots in rural Kashubia, marries Hedwig Lemke and casts his lot in with the Poles, going to work for the Polish Post Office in the post-World War I Free City of Danzig. Despite their differing political allegiances, the three, Jan Bronski, Alfred Matzerath, and Agnes, always appear together in snapshots that serve Oskar as a guide to his family history. The two men, different as they were and despite Jan's marriage to Hedwig, are united in their love of Agnes. To be sure, it is Alfred whom she marries, but she and Jan "were steeped in adultery from the very first day of Mama's marriage." Oskar, born in September 1924, is effectively the product of this trinity, with Jan as well as Alfred, Alfred as well as Jan, his putative father.

With the assistance of a midwife, Oskar is born under two sixty-watt light bulbs. Clairaudient—that is, capable of hearing what is not present to the ear—and with his mental development completed at birth and needing only a little filling in, Oskar from that moment "took a very critical attitude toward the first utterances to slip from [his] parents beneath the light bulbs." He decides to do certain things in life and not do other things. He combines an utterance of his mother, "When little Oskar is three, he will have a toy drum," with his perception of a moth persistently hitting the light bulb, chattering against the bulb as if to unburden itself, as if the dialogue with the light were its last confession. In short, the moth is "drumming," and is thereby Oskar's master. It is only the prospect of receiving his drum in three years that prevents him from giving stronger vent to his desire to have nothing to do with the world, to return to the womb as a rejection of the world and of Matzerath's joyous plans for Oskar's later participation in the running of the family grocery store.

On his third birthday, a sunny September day, Oskar receives his tin drum with its band of serrated red and white; the event is commemorated in a full-length portrait photo. On the occasion of the photo, Oskar reiterates even more forcefully his resolution not to become a grocer, adding a similar absolute refusal to become a politician. So profound is his loathing of the world of adults of the lower middle class who could not and never would understand him that he then and there resolves to remain as he is—that is, not to grow any more. How to realize that resolution? By arranging an accident in which he would fall through a trap door carelessly left open down into basement warehouse of the grocery store. The plunge is a complete success. Upon recovering from his injuries, unspecified except that his head bled but in any case requiring four weeks in the hospital, Oskar ceases to grow any further. His height remains fixed at three feet, one inch. He begins to drum.

The cheap toy wears out after four weeks of drumming in protest at the world, both on the streets of Danzig and in the Matzerath home. The tin has broken off into the inside of the drum where it clatters away, while Oskar's drumming wrists are dangerously close to the jagged edges. Although his mother has a certain sympathy for him, his "father" does not. Moreover, after Oskar's damaging plunge through the carelessly left-open trap door, Matzerath is doubly sensitive to any danger to his presumed son. He tries to take the drum away. Oskar lets loose a glass-shattering shriek, destroying the front of a grandfather's clock. In this way an incredulous Oskar learns that he can use his voice to protect his drum from those who would take it.

Oskar uses his drumming talent defensively at first. When the neighborhood children—their names, including that of the redoubtable Susi Kater, are still unknown to us—are playing such games as "Where's the Witch, black as pitch?" Oskar professes unconcern, but picks up the rhythm of their jingle as he marches down the street, drumming. Similarly, he uses his unique vocal talent defensively at first, but later "out of pure playfulness"—that is, destructively. As early Nazism increases around him, his glass-shattering becomes increasingly destructive. The most sensational episode of art for art's sake, as Oskar calls it, occurs when he climbs to the top of the 150-foot Stockturm, a brick tower giving a panoramic view of Danzig, and lets out a shriek that spectacularly bursts the windows and doors of the nearby municipal theater. The beginning of the next chapter, an abrupt narrative switch in time to 1952-1954, contains a withering denunciation of the consuming society in postwar West Germany, underlining the fact that the novel is, among other things, political in intent.

From his seventh to tenth years, Oskar wears out a drum every two weeks. His source of replacement is the toy store run by Sigismund Markus, a Jew. Markus is an admirer of Oskar's mother Agnes, but although she is friendly with Markus she reserves her extramarital affection, as Oskar is well aware, for rendezvous with Jan Bronski. Nothing escapes Oskar, including Jan's indefatigable fondling of Agnes, sometimes almost under Alfred Matzerath's eyes.

In August 1935, just short of his eleventh birthday, Oskar plays his drum at a huge outdoor Nazi rally, such as were increasingly frequent in the mid-thirties. Oskar plays not as a guest, but as a crasher, and not out in the open, but underneath the platform. As a prominent Nazi party official approaches, accompanied by a complement of storm troopers, march music is quite obviously called for. But Oskar strikes up a waltz tempo. He plays insistently, and at a crucial moment his rhythm is picked up by the official drummers. A clarinetist plays the melody of "The Blue Danube" waltz. As the Nazi dignitaries rage, men and women begin dancing Viennese waltzes on the meadow. The rally disintegrates; a rainstorm completes its dissolution. The special significance of the waltz used to break up the Nazi rally lies in Hitler's known hatred of the waltz: "a stupid waste of time and these Viennese waltzes are too effeminate for a man to dance."[2]

At the age of fourteen Oskar frequently accompanies his mother to church confessions that barely keep pace with her adulteries with Jan Bronski. There Oskar observes a striking physical resemblance between himself and a plaster Christ-child seated in a Virgin Mary's lap. But can the Christ-child drum as well as Oskar? Oskar puts the drum cord around His neck, the drumsticks in His hands, and challenges the Christ-child to a drumming contest. If Christ can do everything, he ought to be able to drum! Oskar demonstrates. The plaster statue fails to perform. Oskar gives Him a blow to the head.

Oskar's poor mama, Agnes, is pregnant again when the inseparable trinity—Agnes, Jan, and Alfred—accompanied by Oskar and his ubiquitous drum, take a walk on the beach on Good Friday, 1938. They watch as a longshoreman hauls in a clothesline at the end of which is a horse's head, used as bait to trap eels. The longshoreman props open the jaws, forces the eels out, and puts them in a potato sack containing salt, in which they writhe in their death throes. Agnes's face turns chalky white at the spectacle. She vomits her breakfast, attracting seagulls, which even Oskar's drumming cannot disperse.

Alfred Matzerath prepares the eels for cooking and tries to force Agnes to eat them, as Oskar drums away. Although Agnes is pregnant, she is most reluctant to carry on the life cycle by eating eels which, the longshoreman has said, feast not only on horses' heads but also on human corpses. (The reader may infer irony, or even blasphemy, in the relationship of this hint of reincarnation to that implicit in Good Friday.) Agnes, refusing to eat the eels, flees the room, throwing herself on the marital bed. Alfred tries to console her, fails, and summons Jan to "pacify" her. Her composure restored, she returns to the dining room, and eats eel. Not much later, in personal desperation at the rise of Nazism as it affects her—Jan with the Poles, Alfred a Nazi—Agnes commits suicide by the uncontrolled, unremitting eating of fish, of which plenty are at hand in the family grocery.

In a foreshadowing of the infamous "Crystal Night" of November 1938, Oskar two years earlier had shrieked show windows into shards of glass. His action was minor compared to the violence and destruction wrought by the Nazis on Jews, on the synagogue, and on Jewish stores on Crystal Night—named for the broken glass. Among the casualties is Oskar's friend and supplier of drums, the toy merchant Sigismund Markus, whom Oskar finds dead at his desk, along with the dregs of the poison he has taken. Moved, but also concerned about his future supply of drums, Oskar reckons this moment as the end of his childhood.

As book 2 begins, Alfred Matzerath has hired a teenage girl by the name of Maria Truczinski to help him run the grocery store. Oskar has his first sexual experiences with Maria, discovering that a simple seltzer powder in Maria's navel exerts a pronounced aphrodisiac effect on her. Maria is also an adept worker in the grocery store. That and proximity endear her to Alfred Matzerath. She becomes pregnant. At an advanced stage she on one occasion awakens just before Oskar can plunge a pair of scissors into her body. Although Alfred marries her, it is never certain whether Oskar or Alfred is the father of her child Kurt, born in 1941. Oskar believes he is, Alfred believes he is.

Oskar leaves Danzig as part of a theatrical troupe of dwarves led by Bebra, whom he had met some years earlier at a circus. Now with the war on, Bebra is a captain in Special Services, taking his troupe to France to entertain the occupation troops. At first Oskar is not quite sure he wants to join the troupe, but when he is introduced to the lady on Bebra's arm—the three-foot three-inch Roswitha Raguna— he cannot resist. Oskar's theatrical act consists of using his voice to shatter glasses and bottles. Not surprisingly, an affair develops between him and Roswitha, who seems to him at once young and ageless. While the troupe is visiting the fortifications on the coast of Normandy, the Allied invasion begins, and Oskar's beloved Roswitha is killed by a naval artillery shell. Oskar returns to his native Danzig on June 11, 1944, the day before his son's, or possibly his half-brother's, third birthday.

For Kurt's birthday Oskar brings him a red-and-white lacquered tin drum, like his own. Showing no inclination to follow Oskar's path as a drummer, Kurt destroys the instrument and from then on becomes increasingly insufferable to Oskar. Feeling at loose ends at home—"Maria had Matzerath"—Oskar takes up churchgoing. At the same time he becomes the mascot and leader of "The Dusters," a youth gang, such as proliferated in Germany at the close of the war. Oskar, who begins to call himself "Jesus," persuades The Dusters to become churchgoers. While the boys are sawing up a plaster statue of the Virgin Mary, the Christ-child, and John the Baptist, they are surprised and apprehended by the police. In the trial that follows, Oskar palms himself off as an invalid not in possession of his mental faculties. He is acquitted.

By now, December 1944, the German Second Army has taken up defensive positions in the heights surrounding Danzig, and the populace is living in basements. In January the city is burned and occupied by the Russians. With the Matzerath family and friends hiding in the grocery basement and the Russians advancing block by block, Alfred Matzerath is advised that it might be a good idea to remove his Nazi lapel pin. Oskar so contrives matters however that his supposed father is in possession of the damning emblem as the Russians enter. Alfred attempts to swallow the pin. A Kalmuck soldier empties the magazine of his tommy gun on him. Clearly, Nazi Germany is in its final stage.

A coffin to bury Alfred in is fashioned of margarine crates, which however is not so well carpentered as to keep Matzerath's hand from emerging, as Oskar looks on and Kurt throws rocks at the crosses that mark nearby graves. Oskar reminds himself that he is twenty-one years old, without parents, without any more presumptive fathers. He ponders whether or not to throw his drum into Matzerath's grave: "should I or shouldn't I?" He decides he should. As the third shovelful of sand covers the drum, Oskar, suffering a severe nosebleed, begins to grow. Only in an apparent throw-away line in the following chapter does Oskar let the reader know that one of Kurt's stones, finding a target other than crosses, has hit him in the back of the head: "It was only [then] that I began to grow." It is a curious and perhaps significant point, since it is Grass's way of reminding the reader of Oskar's degree of sanity or insanity and thus his reliability as a narrator.

Oskar, Maria, and Kurt join the throng of refugees on a freight train leaving Danzig and Kashubia for the West. After Polish soldiers throw a bale of straw into each car, at approximately 11 A.M. on June 12, 1945, the train pulls out of Danzig, which is already being called Gdańsk. Oskar painfully grows en route, three and a half to four inches between Danzig and Stettin, mostly in his legs, only a little in the chest or head. He suffers fever and convulsions, and a hump emerges on his back. Having attained a height just short of four feet, he winds up in the Düsseldorf City Hospital, remaining there from August 1945 to May 1946. In his later asylum refuge, where Oskar prevails on his keeper Bruno to write down some of his autobiography, he finally attains a height of four feet two, the last inch coming while he is telling Bruno about his growth in the freight car coming West.

The third book dwells on Oskar's attempt to integrate himself into a new, adult, bourgeois life in the new post-World War II political entity, West Germany, bereft of both his drum and his ability to shatter glass by shrieking. He tries and abandons night school. He completes an apprenticeship in stonecutting. Wishing to bear responsibility, he provides for Maria and Kurt. Although he sometimes goes out with a nurse Gertrud, he proposes marriage to Maria. She finally declines, hoping, however, that Oskar will remain her friend. In Oskar's opinion Maria's response was really dictated by the West German currency reform of 1948: Maria thrives in the striving, consuming society that was becoming characteristic of the West.

In the meanwhile, having escaped the destiny of a bourgeois husband and entrepreneur, Oskar frequents the Düsseldorf Art Academy, where he picks up fees for modeling. He takes a room near another nurse, Dorothea. As fizz-powder had served the teenage Maria, so a coconut-fiber mat proves aphrodisiac to nurse Dorothea. Now referring to himself (and his penis) as Satan, Oskar proves inadequate to the occasion. Dorothea feels compelled to move away, while Oskar devotes his energies to a jazz band, in which he plays drums.

The band performs in a unique Düsseldorf basement nightclub called the Onion Cellar. It caters especially to those members of the middle class who in 1950 were back on the road to prosperity after the currency reform in West Germany. Because in recent decades the German capacity to cry has been much attenuated, despite more than ample suffering all around, the Onion Cellar provides a meaningful service for its patrons: it distributes onions, to help them shed tears. In his own opinion, Oskar has plenty to cry about: the loss of his fathers, of his poor mother. However, the musicians are contractually prohibited from using onions to cry. In fact, they do not need onions. Oskar's drum helps. He has but to play a few bars and he can cry.

With the recovery of his talent both for drumming and for glass-shattering, Oskar is persuaded to go on a concert tour, including a visit to the Norman coast, where he had performed with Bebra and Roswitha during the Allied landings in World War II. As a proper West German—he has already opened a savings account—Oskar too becomes rich, in his case by becoming a popular recording star.

As the novel draws to a close the reader discovers the nature of the trial that Oskar has cryptically referred to at its beginning. In July 1951 he was walking in a rye field in the suburbs with his rented dog, Lux. Lux, having run off a bit—perhaps wanting to be a dog by himself, Oskar speculates—returns with something between his jaws that proves to be a woman's finger with a ring on it. How or where Lux came by the severed finger is unclear. Oskar in any case is eventually accused of the murder of nurse Dorothea. We learn that the criminal case is to be resumed and that Oskar, in the insane asylum on his thirtieth birthday, is confined only for observation. Not only behind him, but also ahead of him, he recognizes the Black Witch as he summons her by playing the ditty learned on his drums long ago in his childhood from Susi Kater and her backyard gang of eight- to ten-year olds.

The initial and closing scenes of the novel at the insane asylum are not the only occasions on which Oskar picks up the narrative threads of the 1952-1954 period. Such occasions occur rather frequently as Oskar interrupts his 1899-1954 narrative, and the reader is temporarily back in asylum quarters while the latter writes or dictates and, most importantly, discourses on contemporary topics. This is the structural means by which Grass underscores the cyclicity of events or situations, the similarity between an event in, say, 1932 and one in 1953 or 1954. In all-important political-social terms this amounts to underlining a similarity between the pre-Nazi or proto-Nazi or vintage Nazi past and the presumably different—but as Grass is demonstrating, not so different—post-Nazi West Germany.

When Oskar climbs the Danzig Stockturm, for example, toward the end of 1932, to shatter the glass windows and doors of the municipal theater, his apparently irrational rage seems to be directed not toward any affront to him, as was his earlier glass-shattering, but rather in response to the vibrations stirred in him by the rise of Nazism, by the imminence of the Nazi takeover. That takeover in fact occurs in 1933, and its first purely military conquest—that of Poland—occurs in 1939. At the conclusion of the premonitory glass-shattering from the Stockturm the reader is transported to Oskar in his asylum bed, where Oskar declaims against a possible German reconquest of Poland in the early 1950s, fired by revanchism and conducted with the assistance of the prosperity, the consumer goods, and the shallow remorse of the Federal Republic that is, for example, capable of giving former Nazis political office.

*The Tin Drum* is not merely a political simile. It is much richer, much more complex, much more ambiguous than that. As one considers some of the details of this richness, complexity, and ambiguity, it is well to bear in mind that Günter Grass is a political man and a political writer, and that to him, to be a writer means to be an *engaged* writer.

More than one critic reminds us that the title of the novel is *The Tin Drum,* not *The Tin Drummer,* and that the reader should concentrate attention more on the drum and less on the person who beats it. It is certainly true that Grass's book-jacket design of Oskar and the drum contrives, by means of both composition and color, to attract the eye to the drum. Still, to focus all attention on the drum seems a self-limiting approach to a novel bursting with ambiguities—rather like deciding the pervasive Grass egg-chicken conundrum (most concentrated in the poem "In the Egg") in favor of the primacy of the egg because that's in the name of the poem. The drum is different things at different times and different things at the same time. Surely not least, the drum is martial. It symbolizes at once the militaristic Nazi ideology forcing its way from the outside as well as the denunciation of and warning against that ideology working from the inside out by way of Oskar's wrists and drumsticks.

The drum is a musical instrument as well as a symbol of artistic creation. Grass himself is an adept at the drum, having played professionally in a jazz group. To give Oskar his due, he is apparently a good and versatile drummer. One is probably justified in extracting whatever musical metaphor can be usefully applied to a given drumming—as was applied some pages above to the waltz-time drumming at a Nazi rally. (But still, it is a drummer, Oskar, who makes the instrument resound to a three-quarter beat.) As symbols of artistic creation, Oskar's drums are perhaps limited by the fact that his single overriding art is protest. The drum also has sexual connotations: Oskar uses the term "drummings" to describe his sexual intercourse with Maria. And Oskar's drum is silent at the time of his impotence with nurse Dorothea. On the other hand, one would be obliged to consult Freudian dogma to attach sexual importance to Oskar's catalytic desire for a drum on his third birthday.

A mythic interpretation of *The Tin Drum* regards the dwarf Oskar as a demigod and epic hero.[3] To be sure, he is born a mortal, but already he is clairaudient and knows his strengths. On his mother's suggestion of a drum in his future his mind focuses on the full knowledge of the drum's instrumentality to his mission. Oskar's conversations with Jesus and Satan are not the dialogues of a possible lunatic with his alternating alter egos, but rather dialogues between a demigod and mythic powers. The same demigod has access to gods—that is, to Alfred and Agnes Matzerath, Jan Bronski, Maria Truczinski, Sigismund Markus, Bebra, and so on—and his ritual adventures impinge on those gods.

As epic hero and dwarf, Oskar has a decided proclivity toward the subterranean—basements especially. One may also think of bunkers, as on the Norman coast. And in the more general category of concealment there are, for example, Grandmother Anna's skirts, closets, bedrooms, under tables, under Nazi rostrums. In subterranean or hidden places Oskar continually finds renewed strength for his mission of protest. His plunge at age three into the Matzerath basement is the most momentous accumulation of strength for the future. As a primitive demigod his immortality is based on just such a "death"—on going down into the earth, and on renewal, emerging from the earth. Oskar's drum—or drums, for they too require renewal—are the symbol and means of his connection with both his social world and his sacred world. Thus on the one hand he uses his drum to entertain the troops or to make money in show business, while on the other hand he drums up, in the manner of a shaman, the Black Witch that stands before him at the end. Needless to say, within the mythic environment the hero may have recourse to the symbolic qualities of the drum, certainly including the sexual and the invocational. The guarantee and supplement of the drum, Oskar's glass-shattering voice, is quite literally supernatural.

Related to the concept of Oskar as demigod and epic hero is the concept of Oskar as an embodiment of freedom, of power to act at will. This myth requires two assumptions: that the novel, because it is chronological, is also linear; and that it is a picaresque novel, with Oskar as the sovereign picaro, outside society's pale, free to dupe that society.[4] In the first place, though, the novel is not one-dimensionally linear. In the second place, while it can indeed be rewarding to consider Oskar as a picaro, in doing so one may well become persuaded that, as also in the case of mythic hero, he is both that and more, both that and something quite different as well. For ambiguity, not singularity, is Grass's mode, and that is as true of his fiction as it is of his drama or poetry.

The picaro, whose antecedence in western Europe goes back to Spain of the sixteenth and seventeenth centuries, is a skeptical outsider, quite free of the burden of principle, not to mention that of bourgeois morality. ( *Lazarillo de Tormes* [1554], of unknown authorship, and *Guzmán de Alfarache* [1599], by Mateo Alemán, are prototypical examples.) The picaro's character is static, he or she (there are *picaras* too) is an astute observer and trickster more than a doer. The picaro characteristically feigns ignorance to mask his cleverness. A picaresque novel is the biography (usually the autobiography) of such a wandering rogue as he undergoes adventures with a cross section of society, the adventures being recounted ironically or satirically.

Oskar, or at least some of Oskar, reflects many of these picaresque characteristics. He is an outsider. Even beyond that, he is a loner with very few consistent affective relationships—with Grandmother Anna, for example. If Oskar's status as an outsider, if his detachment should be threatened, he can take recourse to his drum to reestablish that picaresque essential. Oskar gets by, he survives, usually with a measure of duplicity. For example, he emerges unscathed from the battle at the Polish Post Office that results in the death of his father, Jan Bronski; he alone of The Dusters escapes punishment; he walks away whistling from the fiasco that he and his drums make of the Nazi party rally.

The picaro's adventures in a variety of social levels and situations lead to his playing a variety of roles, to which he adapts with the versatility of a chameleon. Oskar even adapts to those features of his hated, native lower-middle-class society that give him protection, or pleasure. His supreme role adaptation is to that of being forever three years old. He exploits this role to the full, and it serves him well as long as he is picaro enough to preserve his detachment, his lack of involvement.

The trouble with Oskar as a picaro is that he can't very well protest beyond a certain point without becoming involved—emotionally involved, including suffering—and when that stage is reached his status as a picaro is compromised. The first striking instance of emotional involvement—as distinguished from a continuing affective relationship—is at the death of his mother, at which his pain is laid bare. His ironic phrase from birth, "my poor mama," becomes straightforward in his pain. There have been other, less verbal, indications of Oskar's capacity or obligation to suffer. While his glass-shattering voice is proof against the designs of adults, it has no power against children. Oskar is revealingly helpless against the backyard gang led by Susi Kater. Not only do the gang members physically force Oskar to ingest the foul concoction they have brewed up, but with their ditty they invoke the Black Witch. Oskar also is made to suffer a whipping at the hands of his presumed son Kurt on the latter's third birthday. Indeed Kurt's continuing refusal to follow Oskar's footsteps, Kurt's inclination to be a follower within society rather than an outsider, is a continuing source of increased suffering for Oskar.

Quite likely the greatest source of emotional involvement and unabashed suffering lies in Oskar's relationship with Maria. He is thrown into a violent if powerless fury when he finds his supposed father Alfred having sexual intercourse with her. His subsequent punching of Maria, as well as his inchoate attempt to stab her in the belly with a pair of scissors, are measures of the intensity of his emotional hurt. His suffering is hardly diminished by her sensible refusal of his later marriage proposal.

Oskar's loneliness as an outsider, far from sharpening his wits, as would be the case with a consistent picaro, seems to condemn him to increasing inability to cope, to increasing guilt, to increasing unherolike impotence (as with nurse Dorothea) and bungling, thus suffering. Small wonder that he takes walks in the fields with a dog. Even this lonely pastime, with the unearthing of the ring finger, brings him further pain. For however much he may wish to return to his earlier relatively value-free existence as an ostensible three-year-old, as a picaro, or even as a fetus, he cannot.

Oskar is referred to as an adapter to various roles. Certainly—to extend the theatrical metaphor—he is given to play-acting, to feigning for effect. Nor is all his acting confined to roles off the stage; he actually goes on the stage as a performer. (His performance *under* the stage is an ironic harbinger.) The novel itself is clearly not a drama, but it contains a drama. Several pages of a chapter in book 2, "Inspector of Concrete, or Barbaric, Mystical, Bored," are written as drama, a reminder, if we need one, that Grass was a dramatist before he was a writer of fiction. Books 1 and 2 of the novel obviously contain a movie, which now exists. All of which suggests that, among other possibilities, a theatrical interpretation of *The Tin Drum* might also yield its insights.

Among other Oskar roles, all partial, that one needs to consider are Oskar as Jesus and Oskar as Hitler. He conspicuously assigns himself the former. However parodistic, not to say blasphemous, the effect, there are some obvious common features. The question of paternity is problematic in both cases, although in different ways. Childhood precocity characterizes both Jesus and Oskar. There seems to be a physical similarity: Oskar asserts that the plaster statue of the Christ-child is his own "spit and image." One would not go far astray in declaring that Oskar nurtures a love-hate relationship with, at least, the statue of the Christ-child, whom on the one hand he can attempt to teach his drumming art to, whom on the other hand he can whack on the head with a drumstick or destroy with a saw.

With his violence against the Christ-child Oskar is denouncing, in a larger sense, that sort of Catholicism that found an accommodation with what ought to have been anathematic Nazism. Impaired as was the plaster Christ-child's ability as a drummer, both the biblical Jesus and Oskar fulfill a mission that consists essentially of awakening, protesting, and warning of imminent bestiality and catastrophe. One may speculatively carry that joint identity a step further and suggest that in neither instance is much heed paid.

Oskar nowhere proclaims, "I am Hitler," as he does "I am Jesus." It is true, though, that both Hitler and Oskar write autobiographies, and sometimes less than credible auto-biographies. Both Hitler and Oskar are born into the Catholic lower middle class, whose values they reject even as they are shaped by them. Ancestry in both cases is cloudy, and illegitimacy a factor, although in Hitler's case only to the extent that he had an illegitimate half-brother. Both boys have good singing voices, even if Oskar's singing is of a unique sort. Both very early decide on art as a profession, and in both cases that art emerges as a quasi art. The enumeration of common or almost common features could continue, but it is probably clear by now that these are largely fortuitous similarities, many of them commonplaces associated with the German or German-Austrian Catholic lower middle class in the nineteenth and early twentieth centuries. Oskar, whose mission is to denounce Nazism, is no Hitler, if in some ways a parody of Hitler.

If ambiguity is to characterize the overall perception of Oskar, *The Tin Drum,* and the various interpretational possibilities, it would be inconsistent to accept Oskar's autobiography with more credulity than doubt. As narrator of his own actions, his reliability is certainly open to question. The first three or four pages of the novel are suggestive. The first line, in fact, contains a warning signal: how much credence should the reader place in the reports of "an inmate of a mental hospital"? Especially the reports of an apparent misanthrope who sows doubt about his own accuracy, who speculates on ways in which writers may hoodwink their readers?

Oskar at three years of age is in the hospital for a month, and a patient at home after that, all as a consequence of his apparently deliberate plunge through the trap door to the basement for the purpose of gaining a plausible explanation for his arrested growth. Oskar's convalescence was not a brief one. What if the supposed accident was a genuine accident? The alternative assumption would make the reader skeptical about taking the autobiographical word of an inmate of a mental institution whose mind is possibly arrested at the level of a three-year-old.

As to his resumption of growth after throwing his drum into Matzerath's grave, Oskar's testimony is even more ambiguous. At first, the reader is given to understand that it is the burial of the drum and Oskar's concomitant resolution to grow that are effective. Only significantly later, in another chapter, does Oskar attribute his renewed growth to the blow on the back of the head by a rock. The movie, given Grass's aversion to flashbacks, treats the episode in such a way that Kurt makes a prophet (ironically?) of his perhaps deranged putative father. Oskar, looking at the sand covering his drum, says, "I shall, I must, I will—grow!" At this, Kurt assumes a throwing stance, aims at the back of Oskar's head, throws, and hits the mark. One may well speculate that that trauma contributes as little as the one received in the Matzerath basement to Oskar's narrative reliability.

Bruno Münsterberg, Oskar's keeper in the asylum, intervenes repeatedly in the narration, by no means subtly casting doubt on Oskar's veracity. On the other hand, given the specific warder-and-patient relationship, Bruno has ample reason to take verbal jabs at Oskar while himself presuming to a laudable objectivity. It is true that Oskar often enough contradicts his own reports, for example, his conflicting versions of events at the battle for the Polish Post Office. On the other hand, it is difficult to judge whether "often enough" is enough to qualify Oskar's narrative divagations as pathological rather than run-of-the-mill narrative reembroidering. As elsewhere in the novel, ambiguity prevails. The two chief themes—political, as it happens, or sociopolitical—that rise out of the ambiguity are: disdain for the monstrosity of Nazism; and fear, warning of those elements in West Germany, the comfortable consuming society, that may well contribute to a recurrence of Nazism.

*The Tin Drum* was awarded the prize of Group 47 when it was still an incomplete manuscript in 1958. It has gone on to win acclaim as one of the epochal novels of the Western world and at the same time to become a best-seller with millions of copies in a variety of languages. Combining features of nineteenth-century novel structure with the material and the perceptions of the twentieth century, it proved the reports of the death of the novel to be premature. It resists any single-level interpretation (which might be at once appropriate and deficient) because its mode is that of highly developed ambiguity. Perhaps the single most pervasive characteristic (allied with a wealth of others) is that of protest against a monumentally criminal political deformity, supplemented in book 3 by a gathering fear and implicit warning against the recurrence of the deformity. It is an eloquent polemic but, again, far more.

# 3

## Cat and Mouse

The material of the novella *Cat and Mouse* was originally conceived as a chapter of the novel *Dog Years*. The spin-off and completion of *Cat and Mouse,* however, occurred well before Grass completed the novel. Coping with the material of *Cat and Mouse* seems to have inhibited him from the completion of the novel. The latter subsequently proceeded more smoothly as a consequence of the insight that he gained from writing *Cat and Mouse*. The novella was published in September 1961, and exactly two years later the long and complex novel appeared.

The German novella is a rather specialized genre, not merely shorter than a novel, but structurally different. The structure is closed, compressed; the novella focuses on a single decisive narrative element, and that element, in the classical formulation of Goethe, is to be singular—indeed unique—and surprising. A character does not, as in a novel, develop through time and experience but reacts to the decisive narrative event that is placed in his or her way. With his typical indefatigability as a researcher Grass is said "to have immersed himself in the history of the genre" before setting out to develop the material of *Cat and Mouse*.[1] The result is a far cry from the scope and prolixity of the novels by which it is chronologically flanked, *The Tin Drum* before and *Dog Years* after. Whether Grass in *Cat and Mouse* actually complies with the requirements embodied in a puristic concept of the novella is a moot point that evokes critical disunity. What is certain is that *Cat and Mouse* is a virtuoso novella of the rank of Thomas Mann's *Death in Venice* or *Tonio Kröger*.

For one thing, when it comes to purism, *Cat and Mouse* encompasses five and a half years, a rather long, although not necessarily forbiddingly long, period of time for a novella. Those five and a half years are exactly equal to the five and a half years of World War II beginning with the German invasion of Poland in fall 1939 and ending with the final weeks of fighting preceding the Nazi military collapse in spring 1945. The military events of the war comprise a detailed background significantly related to the narrative events taking place in Danzig. Joachim Mahlke, the hero of the story, may appear to have undergone character development over this considerable span of time and events. (Since he is only fourteen years old when the action begins, such development can only be expected.) On the other hand it is arguable that Mahlke's nature is fixed, that he tries desperately to elude its implications—those of the struggle of an outsider for recognition and liberating self-realization—fails, and reverts to his essential and original nature before his presumable death.

Or perhaps it is Heini Pilenz, the fictive narrator, who has changed a bit as the result of recounting the events of Mahlke's life some fifteen to twenty years in the past. Thus Grass lets ambiguity shine through. It is at any rate clear that Pilenz is writing the story as a kind of penance—the words mea culpa occur—imposed by a Father Alban. There is even a kind of ecclestiastical psychotherapy in the act of writing, which certainly aims at change. Still, encouraged by Pilenz's repeated contradictions and self-doubt, to which he himself calls attention, one may prefer to remain skeptical, not only about his possible guilt-induced character modification, but about his reliability as a narrator of the last five years of the life of his admired and detested peer, Joachim Mahlke.

Pilenz, the supposedly unskilled narrator, begins in the middle or at least not at the beginning of the story. The initial word of the story, "and," is preceded by an elision sign. Mahlke's physical abnormality, the focus of the initial episode and the symbol of his "otherness," has been with him for some while before the story begins, although Mahlke has not been especially aware of it. This abnormality is an oversized Adam's apple. That is the "mouse" part of the story's title. The "cat" part, in the opening chapter, is a regular black cat that happens to be walking across the *Schlagball* field where Mahlke and his companions—not really friends—are lying around on the grass between games. (*Schlagball* is a game whose basic principle is somewhat like that of American softball. It is less complex and more violent; runners, for example, are retired by being hit with the ball, rather than being tagged or by reaching base later than the ball.) In the Danzig background, between the cemeteries and the technical university, the crematorium is working. The juxtaposition of school and death is predictive and thematic.

Mahlke is dozing, his Adam's apple bouncing. So huge it casts a moving shadow, it attracts the cat's attention. The cat springs. Or has one of the boys, possibly Pilenz, incited the cat to spring onto the mouse? In the course of the novella Pilenz gives several versions of the episode. Despite his outcry, Mahlke receives only a few minor scratches. For the novella, the attack establishes a thematic polarity between suffering and persecution. The eternal cat, to use Grass's phrase, is the symbol of the world's attack on the eternal mouse—persecutor and victim. In more prosaic, immediate terms, the cat symbolizes Mahlke's bedeviled world, that is, the Conradinum, an elite high school in which he is the rare student of lower middle-class origins, bordering on proletarian.

After the attack on the ball field, Mahlke is relentlessly obsessed to conceal, compensate for, and countervail his "mouse," the symbol of his otherness and thus of his vulnerability. To conceal his Adam's apple he hangs a screwdriver on his neck, a can opener, even a necktie; his "invention" of pompoms to be worn around the neck achieves the status of a popular fashion. None of these recourses succeeds. Some of his strategies are subconscious. In his earlier years a sickly boy, behind his age group physically, Mahlke quickly becomes an accomplished and daring swimmer and diver. He who has been a barely tolerated hanger-on with the gang becomes its admired and envied pacemaker in swimming the considerable distance out to the sunken Polish minesweeper, *Rybitwa,* lying in the bay with its bridge above water.

The minesweeper becomes the gang's summer headquarters during the early years of the war—1940, 1941, 1942—as the boys approach the end of high school and inevitable military service. Mahlke is preeminent among them as the strongest and most courageous. Still, as the victim of his mouse and of his efforts to escape the cat, the world that would persecute him, he remains more an outsider than a leader. While the other boys disport themselves amiably, not infrequently in innocent masturbatory fashion or in eating seagull excrement, Mahlke dives and swims his way through the underwater entrance into the boat's radio shack, most of the interior of which lies above the level of the water. Into this private refuge he gradually imports the trappings of his room at home. It thus becomes his home away from the drab home he shares with his widowed mother and his aunt. (Mahlke's father, a locomotive engineer, died in a heroic attempt to forestall loss óf other lives by a runaway locomotive.)

Mahlke transfers to the radio shack his books, food, cooking utensils, record player, and, most importantly, a picture of the Virgin Mary. In his flight from the world he sets up his counterworld in the bowels of the minesweeper, and the queen of his counterworld is the Virgin Mary. Not that Mahlke is even a devout Catholic. His observation of the forms, while correct, is only nominal. The religion as a whole he regards as nonsense, God as a "swindle." "The only thing I believe in is the Virgin Mary." This belief encompasses Mahlke's full range of fantasy, including, increasingly, sexual fantasy. For all his worship of her, though, she has so far proved as unable as any other agent to get the cat off his mouse.

In the fifth of thirteen chapters, the Conradinum, the center of Mahlke's nonminesweeper world (and a politicized microcosm of Nazism) is visited by one of its graduates, an air-force fighter pilot who has been awarded an Iron Cross for his valor in battle. The school invites him to give a speech to the student body. At this point Mahlke is desperate for salvation. Winter precludes him from his sanctum in the minesweeper. And his decoys for his Adam's apple, most recently the pompoms, are losing their efficacy.

As the young air-force hero, wearing his Iron Cross, gives his unconscious parody of all war heroes' speeches, Mahlke, his ears blood-red with excitement, throws his ineffective pompoms to the floor. A new potential salvation is in view: the Iron Cross as protector of the mouse against the cat. Declining to join in the thunderous applause accorded the returned hero, Mahlke, who never sweats, now nevertheless sweats, and with emotion. His emotion is doubtless caused by the paradox with which he now finds himself confronted. Essentially a humanitarian in the mold of his father, and of the Virgin Mary too, he has recognized war as the means by which he may attain the Iron Cross that will still the eternal cat. His idée fixe has found its ultimate focus.

The seventh chapter marks not only the numerical but also the narrative midpoint of *Cat and Mouse*. It has been exactly prefigured in the speech of the air-force lieutenant and in Mahlke's hectic reaction to it, now six months past.

Another alumnus hero, this time a submarine commander, returns to the Conradinum. Another reunion with Nazi ideologues on the faculty. An even closer identification of the school-sport-war triad. Needless to say, the returned naval hero also sports an Iron Cross. Mahlke is reluctant to go the speech. He has to be virtually dragged to it by Pilenz, who significantly notes that he thereby hopes to get the upper hand over Mahlke. It has become increasingly apparent that the narrator Pilenz is an extremely important part of the cat, the school, and the world that is out to get Mahlke. In a signal version of the opening episode of the novella, Pilenz puts forward the suggestion that it was perhaps he who set the cat on Mahlke's mouse.

The speech of the lieutenant commander, wearing his Iron Cross, is an even grosser parody than that of his predecessor, the air-force lieutenant. After a colorless overview of the history of German submarine warfare and a laconic description of his own trumph, he launches into an embarrassingly verbose and romanticized description of nature on the deep. If Mahlke hardly has ears for the incongruous blend of war and nature, he has eyes for the Iron Cross hanging against the naval hero's unbelievable white shirt, spectacle enough to make Mahlke tremble and fear that he has been "recognized." Recognized, that is, as eager to obtain an Iron Cross. He has not long to wait, although the Iron Cross he obtains is not his own.

It is that of the lieutenant commander. Mahlke steals it from the locker room. A search fails to turn up the stolen medal, the "thing," to which both Pilenz and Grass consistently refuse to give a name. Mahlke, who has come to school with an open collar, now gives what Pilenz calls his "necktie premiere." Under his necktie, under his pushed-up collar, is the submarine commander's Iron Cross, the "lozenge." At last Mahlke's Adam's apple, his "motor and brake, had found its exact counterweight."

But Mahlke, who even in his continual travail does not countenance dishonesty in himself—let alone at the end of his travail—goes to the principal of the Conradinum and confesses his theft. In taking this step he ignores Pilenz's dissuasive efforts and puts himself in the power of the principal, Klohse, a Nazi functionary who can, and does, ruin him. Klohse summarily expels Mahlke. As a rare near-proletarian in an elite school, Mahlke can expect to find his fate decisively altered by this irrevocable expulsion, ironically the reward for his honesty. He transfers to another school called, with Grassian irony but by no means implausibly, the Horst Wessel High School. (Horst Wessel [1907-1930] was a Nazi thug slain by Communists out of jealousy over a prostitute he was living with. He was not a pimp, however, as his slayers asserted. The Nazis converted the unsavory affair into a propaganda triumph; the official Nazi song was called *The Horst Wessel Song.*)

Mahlke is not much longer for any school, however. During the summer he volunteers for premilitary training. When he returns he surprises Pilenz with his free and easy manner, quite unlike his former awkwardness. He evidently sees himself on the brink of liberation by having volunteered for the tank corps, "the only branch that still has a chance"— a chance of producing for him the coveted Iron Cross. His mouse is already assuaged by the very prospect of being assuaged, even if Mahlke inwardly is no more disposed to the wanton destructiveness of war than he ever was.

After a period with the Compulsory Labor Service and an astounding sexual relationship with his commanding officer's wife, Mahlke joins the tank corps on the Russian front. Beginning as a simple gun layer, he rises rapidly to sergeant and tank commander. He compiles a brilliant record as a destroyer of Russian tanks; the destructive feats of the erstwhile peace-loving Mahlke are recounted in the newspaper. Mahlke, the hero, is awarded the Iron Cross, and his "chronic throat troubles" are over at last. He returns to Danzig on furlough, to the Conradinum, his speech ready. For he aims to follow the precedent of the two previous alumni heroes who played decisive roles in setting him on the course that has finally assuaged his mouse.

His blithe self-confidence is betrayed. His return to school is not to be a triumph. The stuffed specimen cat, crouching in a glass case at the school, is triumphant. Klohse, the principal, coolly refuses to let Mahlke take his honors. No honors for a former thief. Perhaps over at the Horst Wessel School . . . ? That isn't what Mahlke has in mind. From the beginning his goal has been triumph in the auditorium of the Conradinum. To Klohse's further suggestion that perhaps silence was his best recourse he responds by waylaying the principal on the thorn-tunneled cul-de-sac on which the latter lives and silently striking him in the face. From now on, the Great Mahlke—long so-called by Pilenz—is a fugitive, and not only for overstaying his furlough. His tragic isolation is complete in every sense, for he has no inkling of the moral propriety of his response to Klohse. Mahlke wanders the streets irresolutely. His only companion is Pilenz, who at long last has the upper hand in their ambivalent and failed relationship. Pilenz will betray Mahlke.

Mahlke, ever outwardly devout, repairs to church the next morning, where his crisis of fear is again demonstrated by profuse sweating. Father Gusewski nonetheless fails to ask the humane question, "What's wrong, can I help you?" But in fact Mahlke is beyond help, as Pilenz has told us repeatedly. As if to make that judgment come true, Pilenz declines to hide the fugitive in the Pilenz basement. Instead, although the season is anything but propitious, he suggests that Mahlke hide in the minesweeper in the bay. Although Pilenz's plan is only dimly formulated as to detail, he apparently anticipates doing in his companion and enemy— never his friend—at the seat of the Great Mahlke's youthful preeminence.

At Mahlke's house Pilenz obtains some canned pork together with a can opener. Sweating, he rows at Mahlke's instruction out to the sunken *Rybitwa*. When they arrive on the bridge, Mahlke removes his Iron Cross from his back pocket, hangs it around his neck, humming a selection from the litany, and greets as brothers the chorus of seagulls flying their patterns about the wreck. Having taken off and carefully folded his uniform, as army regulations prescribe, he stands in his red gym pants, survivors of his days at the Conradinum. Then, laden with his two cans of pork, he dives to the underwater entrance to the radio shack, his old refuge and kingdom. But the can opener remains on deck under Pilenz's foot. A moment later Pilenz bangs on the side of the boat, yelling "Can opener!" No answer; he rows back to shore.

After the war Pilenz attends every circus in town to find Mahlke, for one of Mahlke's ambitions was to become a clown. No one knows of any Mahlke. In 1959 in Regensburg Pilenz goes to a meeting of holders of the Iron Cross and has Sergeant Mahlke paged. No response.

Did Mahlke drown or survive? Probably the former. The ending of *this* novella, however implicative, is open, even as its beginning was open: who, if anyone, egged the cat to jump onto Mahlke's mouse? Similarly, the entire course of the novella is in a sense open. Pilenz not only is unsure about narrative details but he is by his own account ignorant of the inner life of his hero. For all his involvement with and commitment to his admired and hated cynosure, Pilenz has no idea what goes on inside Mahlke. Openness—or alternatively, obliqueness—is thus an insistent theme.

A second, equally important theme, is that of Mahlke's unhappy quest. From his awkward and sickly boyhood, before he learned to "swim himself free," Mahlke is on a continual quest to integrate himself as outsider into the society that surrounds him. Initially his quest is to be one of the gang. In this endeavor he pushes himself doggedly through swimming instruction to emerge not just as a competent swimmer but as the best swimmer of all. It is in this endeavor—to be the best—that Mahlke also comes to excel in gymnastics. It is in this endeavor too that Mahlke, who has held aloof from the masturbation practiced by the other boys on the deck of the minesweeper, finally allows himself to be incited by Tulla Pokriefke, the female mascot of the gang, to betray his standards and join in the competition. Characteristically, having joined, Mahlke excels.

The onanistic "Olympiad" scene aboard *Rybitwa* brought the wrath of public moral outrage down on Günter Grass's head. Lawsuits loomed, and he was denounced as a pornographer and a menace to youth. Yet the celebrated fictional episode is anything but gratuitous, which would seem to be a legal prerequisite for pornography. In fact the episode is narratively and thematically crucial to Grass's tale. First, as we have seen and as Grass specifically suggests, it integrates Mahlke into his society. In doing so, it reiterates the motif of his swimming exploits and prefigures the ultimate perversion of his integrative quest—that is, his confrontation with, and adaptation to, Nazism. Second, in regarding the society of boys on the minesweeper as a microcosm of Nazism into which they will all soon be swept, the masturbation becomes a concomitant if not a result of boredom in a society that specifically suppresses individualism, creativity, and humanism. The practice is as inherently sterile as the credo.

In the third place, the aspect of sterility is brought together with the motif of the cyclicity of excrement, decay, and food. This is illustrated by the seagulls that swoop in labyrinthine patterns about the wreck and by their perdurable excrement that accumulates on the boat, tougher than the rust-prone metal to which it adheres. The boys, excepting Mahlke, chip the excrement loose, chew the stuff, spit it mixed with their saliva into the air, where the gulls unknowingly gulp as food the composite of spit and their own excrement. The gulls are no less eager to pluck Mahlke's semen from the smooth sea, crying for more.

Tulla, the only girl on board, non-Catholic and admiring, wants to know if Catholic Mahlke will confess his sin. Of course he will. He takes his Catholicism whole—nonsensical though it may be to him—as the accompaniment to his

Mariolatry. He may not believe in the religion as a whole, he may think it rubbish, but he is outwardly true to it, even as his excessive worship of the Virgin Mary takes on blasphemously erotic qualities. These qualities share the characteristic of grotesqueness with the rapprochement that Mahlke effects with the Nazi state. The two streams, that of Mariolatry and that of an unnatural personal fusing with Nazism, flow together when Mahlke enters the military to serve on the Russian front.

Mahlke serves with distinction, with excellence. If one has noted well the direction of his Mariolatry, one is perhaps prepared for his employment of the Virgin Mary as the means of his astounding and well publicized successes as tank commander and hero. In this role he blasts countless Russian tanks into quiescence by a tactic located not in a training manual but in the heart of his own torment.

Done *for* the Virgin Mary, Mahlke's feats are accomplished also *with* the Virgin Mary—not, however, in the usual manner of divine intervention on the battlefield, but in a shocking parody of that staple form of military aid. As in church Mahlke's gaze at the image of the Virgin Mary is directed to the "belly of the Mother of God," so on the bed of the battlefield before each Russian tank he imagines a vision of the Virgin Mary, at whose womb he directs the phallic cannon of his tank.[2] It is for his unending string of successes based on this distinctive gun-laying technique that Mahlke receives his Iron Cross.

Similar to Oskar Matzerath in *The Tin Drum*, Joachim Mahlke conveys the impression in certain outward aspects of being a caricature of Hitler. The lower middle-class origin, the fatherless adolescence, the dubious relationship to Catholic heritage are obvious points of likeness. More visually striking is the distinctive hair style affected by both Mahlke and Hitler, parted in the center and plastered smooth on the sides. The narrator directs the reader's attention to Mahlke's hair style often enough to stress clearly its resemblance to Hitler's.

Keeping in mind Grass's ambiguity, one may find it still more rewarding, especially in consideration of the ambiguity or paradox that results from the juxtaposition with Mahlke's Mariolatry, to consider Mahlke as a Christ-figure, a Redeemer. Thus Mahlke's steadfastness against temptation, insufficient as it proves, may be compared to the more tenacious steadfastnes of Christ. One may find in Christ's Passion an illumination of Mahlke's extended suffering. Further, Mahlke's long betrayal by Pilenz, the whole topos of the mouse and the cat, finds a suggestive parallel in Christ's betrayal by Judas.

The caricature of Hitler and the reflection (and also caricature?) of Christ are inferential, hinted at, to some extent plausible, but not stated in plain terms by Grass. On the other hand, a Mahlkeian motif that is stated in plain terms, and often, is that of clown. With his unusual physical appearance, his variety of outlandish props to hide the outsize Adam's apple, "a comic figure," source of his companions' repeated outbursts of laughter, Mahlke is a clown-type beyond doubt. To be a circus clown is his stated and restated ambition; he performs his acts, his tricks, and his effects for approval and applause. As a performer he is constantly impelled to outdo himself, to strive in the face of handicap and failure for more and ever more impressive feats. Doubtless his military feats are his supreme gesture before his final clown act, his descent into the minesweeper without his can opener.

Seen in this light, or even that of a compulsive Mariolatry, Mahlke's award-winning destruction of Russian tanks amounts to courage unmasked, heroism revealed as something less grand than is given out in press releases. Mahlke's courage thus unmasked is the centerpiece of a broader unmasking of the military as a whole. The most prominent sidepieces, or more accurately forepieces, of this debunking we have already seen in the unwittingly parodistic speeches given by the fighter pilot and the submarine commander before the students and faculty of the Conradinum.

The Conradinum itself, together with the Church, the continuing focus of Mahlke's feelings, likewise undergoes unmasking. Although ostensibly a humanistic institution, which ought to have responded to and nurtured Mahlke's humanistic inclinations, the Conradinum has fallen completely—or all but completely—under the brutalizing sway of Nazism. Although there are on its faculty ineffective representatives of the school's original humanistic mission, it is not by accident that its present principal, Mahlke's antagonist and, briefly, victim, is a Nazi functionary.

The Catholic Church is the third member of Grass's mercilessly unmasked triad of institutional corruption: military, educational, and religious. The Church is not to be deemed corrupt because Mahlke perverts one of its divine objects of worship, the Virgin Mary, but rather because, like the school, in its appropriation to the nefarious purposes of the Nazi political state, the Church fails its historical, saving mission vis-à-vis the individual who is Mahlike. Father Gusewing, whose languidly homosexual inclinations toward the teenage boys of his parish perhaps suggest the self-serving corruptibility of the institution he represents, changes his name to the more German-sounding Gusewing to ingratiate himself with the hyper-German state. The same Gusewski is pleased to have Mahlke assist him in the services over a period of years. But when Mahlke the war hero is brought down by his nonreception at the Conradinum, when he retaliates against his tormentor Klohse, and becomes a sobbing fugitive taking communion, Gusewski/Gusewing is content to let his sorely tried communicant depart in the rain, while the churchman reflects that maybe he ought to ask Mahlke back in, but.... So much for humane, or even religious, compassion. It is still raining when Pilenz and Mahlke make the final trip to the minesweeper. Rain, Pilenz has been assuring us with cliché-like insistence, brings people together. On the contrary, rain, too, alienates.

Considered from the vantage point of two decades and more after its appearance, *Cat and Mouse* remains a novella of superb craftsmanship and effectiveness. In its more trenchant, surely no less artistic way, it is as stinging, even as savage an indictment of Nazism as that delivered by *The Tin Drum*. It may be that one is more moved to outrage by the shorter work; on the other hand the somewhat less multifarious symbology of the shorter work probably produces a more rapid outrage. But note well—and as with *The Tin Drum*—in *Cat and Mouse* one is not dealing with a tract but with a complex, profoundly moving work of art.

## Dog Years

*Dog Years* is the third and concluding work in The Danzig Trilogy. Like *The Tin Drum* it is a novel of considerable length and rich texture, "a dismal, complicated story," in the judgment of Heini Pilenz, the fictive narrator of *Cat and Mouse*. Not perhaps quite as dismal as the apparent fate of Oskar in *The Tin Drum*, with the Black Witch confronting him; the hero of *Dog Years* emerges as more in control of his fate. Certainly the structure of *Dog Years* is more complicated. If the reader has been alerted to skepticism about accepting the word of Oskar Matzerath and Heini Pilenz, the individual narrators in the Danzig Trilogy, as having a vested interest in obfuscation, Günter Grass now provides in *Dog Years* the aggregate resources of a consortium of narrators, all writing simultaneously according to a timetable that decrees their contributions are to be completed on February 4, 1962. Three—and including Grass himself, four—narrators tell the dismal story of *Dog Years*, each from his own perspective as a participant. It is an ambitious undertaking for the fourth and ultimate narrator, Grass.

One might say *too* ambitious. Inevitably the magnificent *Tin Drum* became the standard by which Grass's subsequent fiction, especially the long novels, are compared. The relatively complicated—but thoroughly controlled and not at all chaotic—narrative structure of *Dog Years* reaped unjustified critical disapproval. It is a fact that *Dog Years* fell far short of its expected popular approval, possibly because of the then unprecedented promotional hyping that preceded and attended its publication. Sales and printings fell off rapidly. Oblivion is hardly the word for a novel that has appeared in half a million copies, more or less. And yet as it has found fewer readers by far than *The Tin Drum*, so has it also found less interpretation. That is regrettable, for it is a powerful novel and a powerful denunciation of Nazism and of the West German tendency, in Grass's clear view of 1963, to suppress or rewrite that criminal chapter in history. (It seems worth noting that *Dog Years* thus preceded the Holocaust revelations by roughly fifteen years.)

The first of its three fictive narrators, Eddi Amsel, the director of the consortium and the hero of the novel, is a half-Jew—thus a Jew in the definition of Nazi racial laws. Amsel ("blackbird" in German) also appears in the novel in a variety of differently named personae. This may at first confuse the reader, especially because Amsel's identity with his primary persona, the mine owner Brauxel, is merely alluded to in the early part of the novel and only much later stated outright. It is not unfitting then, in the ambience of a potash mine, that Amsel/Brauxel's contribution to the novel is called "Morning Shifts." (The German word *Frühschichten* means "morning shifts" as well as "early strata," as in geology. The author of "Morning Shifts" is also laying the foundation, the basic layers, of the novel.) Amsel's report covers the period from his birth in 1917 until 1927. However he begins narratively with 1925 before backing up, in the "Fifth Morning Shift," to his birth.

The fictive writer of the second section of the novel is Harry Liebenau, an aesthete, a failed poet, now working in radio broadcasting, and an able, even facile writer. His contributions to the novel are "Love Letters," written to his cousin Tulla Pokriefke. The "letters" are for the most part only called that; they are extended reminiscences rather than communicative correspondence. And in any case Harry Liebenau is writing them for the director of the writing project, Eddi Amsel, and not for Tulla. We may remember Tulla from *Cat and Mouse*. She has grown up to be a thoroughly unpleasant, not to say diabolical woman, something like a human Black Witch. Harry Liebenau, despite fictive authorship of about 50 percent of the novel, plays little role *in* the novel. His "letters"to Tulla report on or evoke events from 1922 to 1945. Toward the end of Harry's section, Günter Grass himself intervenes, apparently fed up with Harry's skillful but noncommittal prose, with his refusal to come to grips with the outrages to which he aseptically refers.

The third fictive author is Walter Matern, who with revealing egotism calls his section "Materniads." ("Materniads" as well as "Morning Shifts" probably also reflects the titling tendencies of Jean Paul [Jean Paul Friedrich Richter, 1763-1825] and Hans Jacob Christoffel von Grimmelshausen [about 1622-1676], two of Grass's favorite German writers.) Matern, physically powerful, coarse, unreflective, often irrational, German (but, ironically, of remote Polish descent), is the counterpart to his friend and occasional victim, Amsel, who is fat, weak, refined, intellectual, rational, and half Jewish. Their rivalry, their love-hate relationship, provides the principal narrative thread of the novel, beginning when they are both eight-year-olds on the banks of the Vistula River near Danzig. Matern, a teeth-grinding actor, called the Grinder (his father is a miller), narrates the post-World War II era from 1946 until May 1957. If Liebenau confronts the past by glib avoidance, Matern confronts it and his guilt in it by suppression. He uses the present tense for past events not so much for the sake of vividness but to distance himself from it.

At the age of eight the clever, observant Eddi Amsel and the physical Walter Matern, frequently typified as a fist, swear blood brotherhood to each other. Shortly thereafter Matern, chafing at a relationship in which Amsel is dominant in every respect but the physical, throws the pocketknife used in the oath of brotherhood into the Vistula. The parable-like motif, to recur at the end of the novel, is concluded by a bet: will Matern accept a new knife from Amsel? Amsel bets he will, Matern bets he won't. The implication of the oath, of the gift of the knife, of the rebellious disposal of the knife, of the bet, is that the German and the Jew share a troubled and ambivalent friendship. This is one of the two chief themes of *Dog Years*. The second is referred to in the title of the novel, developed initially in Amsel/ Brauxel's "Fifth Morning Shift," and depicted in a startling jacket illustration of a dog by Günter Grass.

The jacket illustration shows a black skeletal human hand so arranged as to create a shadow profile of the head of an alert, aggressive black Alsatian wolf dog (German shepherd), with a red tongue protruding from its mouth that suggests at once a sausage, a penis, and excrement. In the "Fifth Morning Shift" occurs a canine lineage in the style of biblical parody: "And Perkun sired Senta; and Senta whelped Harras; and Harras sired Prinz; and Prinz made history." Further, the progenitor "Perkun's grandmother on her father's side had been a Lithuanian, Russian, or Polish she-wolf." The ultimate descendant of this partly lupine lineage, Prinz, makes fictional history as Adolf Hitler's dog. (The dog-lover Hitler did in fact own a much beloved Alsatian, originally a gift from his associate Martin Bormann. It was a bitch, however, named Blondi, and in pictures, at least, she seems to justify the name.)

The Dog Years of the title are the years embraced by Perkun and his tribe, with emphasis on the period from Senta, the dog of the Matern family, onwards—the years during which Nazism incubated and flourished. Dog Years also suggests a decades-long extension of "dog days," from the beginning of July through mid-August, when Sirius, the dog star, is in the ascendant, and dogs are popularly thought to go mad. Madness, in turn, suggests Nazism.

In addition to the Matern family dog, Amsel/Brauxel tells us about the Matern family, Catholics tracing their lineage back to a famed Polish robber, Materna; about Walter Matern's grandmother; about Walter Matern's Father, a deaf miller, who makes prophecies with the help of mealworms, to which he listens with a deaf but clairaudient ear pressed against a sack of meal.

Brauxel, in 1962 the prosperous owner of a potash mine, is somewhat more expansive about the details of Eddi Amsel's family background. Well he might be, for as the reader suspects, he *is* Eddi Amsel. Eddi's father Albrecht was a Jew, some say of ultimately Dutch provenance—a family of tailors. Albrecht Amsel left the Vistula at the age of sixteen, moving in stages to Berlin. "Fourteen years later he had come—metamorphosed, Protestant, and wealthy—to the Vistula estuary." The point is that the wealthy wholesaler, Albrecht Amsel, has become more German than the Germans. He married a Protestant woman, sang baritone in the church choir, founded an athletic club, became a reserve lieutenant, owned a library devoted to the "great men" of Prussia like Frederick the Great, and fell in the Battle of Verdun in World War I.

Why did Albrecht Amsel make such a lifelong project of denying his Jewishness? First, it was a response to the anti-Semitism of the larger society in which he lived. Second, relatedly, he took as his Bible, so to speak, the notorious book, *Sex and Character* (1903), by the fanatically anti-Semitic Jewish philosopher, Otto Weininger. Weininger's work, commonly found in German middle-class homes of this era, distinguishes two types: "Aryan" (misusing the term), "Germanic," "good"; and "Jewish," "negative," "bad." Weininger goes on to specify fanatically Germanness in a way that anticipates Richard Wagner or Adolf Hitler— or Albrecht Amsel. The goal for a Jew is to overcome the inherently negative attributes of Jewishness and adopt the inherently positive ones of Germanness. Brauxel admits: "Weininger has grafted quite a few ideas on the present writer. The scarecrow is created in man's image." The first sentence of Brauxel's admission contains one of several implications that Brauchsel (he spells his name variously) *is* Eddi Amsel. The second sentence hints at Eddi Amsel's life's work, the building of artistic scarecrows.

Eduard Amsel was born two months after his father's death at Verdun. His latent scarecrow-inventing spirit is known to all the birds even as he is being baptized a Protestant. At the age of five and a half he builds his first scarecrow. He builds his early experimental scarecrows for no other purpose than that of art, yet their verisimilitude is such that they are functional as well. Birds panic, and he makes money. Amsel keeps a diary that records much of his scarecrow-building activity and provides his Brauxel persona with narrative data. After a period during which he dips into Prussian mythology for his scarecrow models, Amsel produces his masterpiece for some time to come. Prompted by the sight of an eagle above a lamb, a metaphor for Prussian militarism as the raptor of the innocent, the artist constructs "The Great Cuckoo Bird . . . tarred, feathered, and superman-high," spreading superstition and terror. It has to be burned. Already afire, the monster makes a last stab at flying before it disintegrates. Thus the parodistic image of Prussian militarism wedded to Nazism is destroyed by fire, the favorite symbolic weapon of Nazism (as in book burning, or the burning of the Reichstag). The artist resolves to build a better scarecrow.

Well into "Love Letters," Harry Liebenau's part of the novel, and after a period of artistic stasis following the destruction of the Great Cuckoo Bird, Amsel creates nine Hitler storm-trooper scarecrows. Each is equipped with an internal mechanism that impels it to march and salute mechanically—that is, like a real-life storm trooper. To receive the salutes of this squad of highly realistic scarecrows,

Amsel mimes Hitler. For that mockery, but also as a consequence of his dominant role in their friendship, he is brutally beaten up by Matern, who has flip-flopped from Marxism to Nazism and is now a storm trooper, actually encouraged by Amsel. Matern is assisted in the early stages of the assault in the snow by nine storm-trooper associates. But he needs little direct help from the uniformed thugs in knocking out all thirty-two of Eddi Amsel's teeth. The battered Amsel leaves Danzig. When he shortly returns, it is as the slim ballet director Hermann Haseloff, with a mouthful of gold, for which reason he is also called Goldmouth.

Haseloff has created a scarecrow ballet to be called *The Scarecrows*, or *The Revolt of the Scarecrows*, or *The Gardener's Daughter and the Scarecrows*. The ballet contains three figures—the gardener's daughter, the downtrodden gardener, and the scarecrow—representing respectively art (danced by the now svelte, formerly fat Jenny Brunies), German society in Amsel's youth, and politics or political ideologists. Jenny's description of the ballet to Harry illuminates the interplay of art, society, and politics, especially the definitive emigration of the scarecrow from the realm of art to the realm of politics. Thus, in Hitler's Germany art is completely identified with totalitarianism. Jenny accomplishes this identification by a mixture of artistic insight and political naiveté, for in fact the pure artist, Jenny, the adopted daughter of an anti-Nazi teacher, cannot understand why art should be censored on external—that is, political—grounds.

The earlier part of "Love Letters," in addition to depicting the lower middle-class milieu of Tulla Polkriefke, also dwells on the roly-poly Jenny Brunies—long before her emergence as a slim prima ballerina—the gypsy adopted daughter of Dr. Oswald Brunies. (Brunies is that rarity in Grass's fiction, a genuine and uncompromised humanist. Denounced for his principles by Tulla, he is sent to an extermination center at neighboring Stutthof.) Jenny

Brunies, who is made to feel Tulla's continual antagonism and eventual violence, aspires to be a ballet dancer in spite of her corpulence. The unlikely comes to pass. Battered by Tulla and her dog Harras, Jenny is metamorphosed into a prima ballerina, while Eddi Amsel is battered and metamorphosed into Haseloff, the ballet director. The batterings occur simultaneously on a snowy winter afternoon. As Matern the Grinder knocks his friend to the snow time and again, not far away Tulla forces Jenny to dance in the snow until she half-collapses, whereupon Tulla repeatedly throws her down till she can no longer get up. These parallel frenzies of violence perpetrated on the innocent may be regarded as the crisis point of the novel: Nazism is revealed.

Like the skilled writer he is, Harry Liebenau deftly interweaves the stories of his relatives, friends, and acquaintances in Danzig as, in their various ways, they subscribe to Nazism—all except Oswald Brunies. "Those who have forgotten," says Liebenau in a rare burst of frankness, "may as well remember." Noting however that he and Tulla had never been to the village of Stutthof, near which lies the extermination camp, he gives us only dry data: the location of the village, its population, the building of the camp, its repeated enlargement, the narrow-gauge railroad connections, even a railroad within the camp. He gives us the history of the area, back to the fourteenth century. Perhaps a grim joke he retells before the history leads to the spareness of the data. The joke is: "They're making soap in Stutthof now, it makes you want to stop washing." The prose stylist Liebenau can come no closer than the data and the grim joke to addressing the heart of the matter of Stutthof.

Günter Grass has to intervene. There is a pile of bones by a factorylike building in the camp at Stutthof, heaped up for the sake of purity—even though, Grass asserts, nothing is pure. Crows wheel over the pile of bones and get fat: "from what?" The crows are the first of four motifs woven into the pile-of-bones sequence, as moving and terrifying a sequence as one is apt to find in any fiction. The second motif is the rats who invade the nearby antiaircraft battery. The rats are clubbed and hooked, brutally and systematically, by the soldiers and auxiliaries, including Liebenau.

But there is a smell hanging over the battery that doesn't come from rats, even the hundreds that are periodically killed, strung up, counted, and buried. The smell is the third motif. Grass mentions the smell frequently, so that the effect is appropriately that of pervasiveness. The fourth motif is the parodistic use of the existentialist jargon of Martin Heidegger, the philosopher who sympathized with the Nazis for a time at the inception of the Nazi power. Heideggerian style is used to relate events of the war, including the rat-killing and the pile of bones. As Störtebeker (who emerges under his real name as Eberhard Starusch in the later novel, *Local Anaesthetic*) says in Heideggerian fashion to Tulla when she wants to bet that the bones are human bones: "The most we can say is that here Being has come into unconcealment."

Tulla is right. To make her point she goes to the pile of bones and brings back a skull. Immediately after this grisly sequence, Grass has the Führer visiting Danzig, receive as a birthday present the dog Prinz, son of Harras. The relationship is obvious. "The dog stands central," asserts Walter Matern, as the first sentence of the first of the "Materniads" that comprise his contribution to the novel. Matern is being released from a POW camp at war's end, and Prinz is his unwelcome companion. Eight days after Hitler's suicide, Prinz had swum across the Elbe River to the future West Germany "and went looking for a new master on the west side of the river." His search ends with his fellow Danziger and follow ex-Nazi, Walter Matern.

Matern narrates the postwar era from his dual perspective as guilty victim and as avenging persecutor of his former Nazi associates who are beginning to live the good life in West Germany. He travels widely in this pursuit, accompanied by the dog, so it is fitting in more than one sense that his headquarters is the men's toilet, with its smell of urine, in the Cologne Central Railway Station. His missions, his posturing missions of retribution tend to take on the form of seducing and/or deflowering the female relatives of his old acquaintances, leaving them either pregnant or infected with venereal disease.

The Grinder, Walter Matern, alternate Marxist and Nazi, is a flawed avenging angel. Accompanied by a satanic dog, who is now generally called Pluto, Matern draws a convenient mantle of forgetfulness over his own crimes as a Nazi, including the disfiguring and disabling of his friend Eddi Amsel. (Amsel, besides losing all his teeth, apparently suffered laryngeal impairment as well, for he speaks forever after in a hoarse voice.) A former actor, Matern gets a job as a radio announcer, but he finds that the radio medium, including such young intellectuals as Harry Liebenau, is already engaged in suppressing Nazi history in favor of confirming the glowing prosperity of the consumer society in West Germany.

Fed up with the west, Matern essays flight to East Germany, the "Peaceloving Camp," in Grass's ironic lexicon. The image of the not-to-be-shaken-off dog races alongside the interzonal train. To change his money more advantageously and more capitalistically, to obtain a razor and blades, two pair of socks, and a change of shirts, Matern briefly detrains in West Berlin, only to be accosted by the dog he would elude and, shortly, by Gouldmouth, who is Amsel/Brauxel/Haseloff. Matern again meets up with the former ballerina, Jenny Brunies, her toes amputated as the result of an injury suffered in an air raid, and now the faded spinster proprietress of Chez Jenny, a nightclub, The four friends—four, because Pluto listens—regale each other with stories.

After the three males have left the club at dawn, Matern with a great windup gesture, throws "the newly recovered pocketknife," yielded up by the Vistula, into the Berlin Landwehr Canal. After he throws, he aims the epithet "Sheeny!" at Goldmouth and, having overreached himself emotionally, sinks to the ground. Characteristically, Matern dominates only in the physical realm, and after the knife was thrown, the relationship once more reverts to one in which Amsel dominates. Amsel/ Goldmouth, "Sheeny," summons a taxi to take the three—himself, Matern, and Pluto—to the airport to catch the first plane for Hanover to visit the nearby underground scarecrow factory of Brauxel & Co. Here in the last "Materniad," called the "Bottom-most Materniad," because the former potash mine, now a scarecrow factory, represents a descent to the deepest levels of the human imagination, Brauxel gives Matern a guided tour. In this scarecrow hell replete with historical and literary allusiveness—not only to Dante's *Inferno*—Matern is baffled and uncomprehending. Finally, in the dressing room up above, as Eddi and Walter step into bathtubs, Walter reflects that "each of us bathes by himself."

Each in his own tub, Eddi and Walter are survivors of the Nazi apocalypse. Eddi Amsel, especially as Brauxel, owner and manager of a scarecrow factory in West Germany, is highly prosperous. In this respect, he is quite unlike his predecessor hero, Oskar Matzerath in *The Tin Drum*, who has survived the Nazi apocalypse neither in body nor (quite likely) in mind.

The symbolically apocalyptic conclusion of *Dog Years*, the hell in the ex-potash mine, is the penultimate conclusion of an apocalyptic motif that is anticipated with the very assignment of a date by which the members of the writing consortium are to hand in their contributions to the manager of the project, Amsel/ Brauxel. That date is February 4, 1962. At the beginning of his own "Twenty-sixth Morning Shift" Amsel/ Brauxel notes that on that date "the critical constellation of the heavenly luminaries calls the world into question." In other words, the waiting needs to be completed before the possible end of the world. A few pages on he observes that the world has after all survived that possible planetarily induced apocalypse. But the inferential question remains throughout the novel: despite the survival of Amsel

and, though less auspicious, of Matern as well, will the world
survive the man-made apocalypse, Nazism? Clearly in 1963
in West Germany Günter Grass had his doubts.

The potential continuing influence of German idealistic
philosophy and Heidegger doesn't help matters. Not only
Liebenau and Störtebeker, but also, and perhaps especially
Matern, longing for a system of belief, succumb to the siren
song of Heidegger. According to Matern, Heidegger's
"words could be swallowed like butter," and Matern is a
victim of the easy swallowing. The militant and arrogant
abstractions in the philosopher's *Being and Time* are suited
to reinforce mental and spiritual vacuity such as that of
Matern in particular or Nazism in general. Obscurity
disguises reality.

Grass's polemic against Heidegger is subject to the
limitation that the reviling is Matern's, not Grass's per se.
However, the parodying, if not the reviling of Heidegger, is
more broadly based and should be regarded as reflecting
Grass. In the event, Grass has been severely criticized for the
denunciation of Heidegger contained in *Dog Years*. And
Grass is notably no friend of German idealistic philosophy,
to which Heidegger is heir. He is an heir who in Grass's eyes
uncritically sanctifies history and, under the pretentious
concept of authenticity, glorifies death and sacrifice—both
of which are on unedifying display in *Dog Years*.

Catholicism hardly fares better. Its bankruptcy, and the
bankruptcy of Christianity as a whole, may be presumed to
be a large contributor to that vacuum of belief into which
Heideggerism rushes. Catholicism certainly fares worse in
*Dog Years* than in *The Tin Drum*. In the latter, Oskar
challenges Jesus to drum, to denounce, to warn, as if there
were some likelihood he would. When Jesus fails to
perform, we may infer that collaboration with Nazism is at
the root. No inference is required in *Dog Years*. Matern's
rejection of Catholicism is as explicit as his accusation that
the Church collaborates. But of course so does he. The
ambivalence is ironic, even dismal.

The connivance of lower middle-class society in abetting Nazism is in *Dog Years* not at all random and almost accidental, as it appeared to be in *The Tin Drum*. Now the connivance is willing, purposeful, and premeditated. In a sense, it seeks Heidegger, who thereupon performs a facilitating function. So insistent is Grass in his accusation and in his demonstration of these points that the novel has been faulted critically for excessive didacticism. But objectivity is perhaps impossible when the topic is Nazism.

In the end, as Walter Matern insists, the dog stands central. The knife-throwing motif structurally connects the beginning of the novel with the conclusion, but the dog is pervasive and thematic. Of half-wild ancestry, from Prussianized territory to the east, the dog is imported to West Prussia, closer to the heart of the country, and there it is nurtured and indulged and glorified and, in brief Maternian remorse, poisoned. Renascent in its offspring, it becomes the Nazi dog par excellence. At the downfall of its Nazi master, it resolves to seek a new master. By now it is transmuted into Pluto, the dog of hell, and it proves not at all an alien in West Germany. It is left at the end chained in Brauxel's underground scarecrow factory as the proper guardian of the undergroud realm, hell. But unchained?

With its multiple themes converging on the central topic, Nazism, with its multiple narration that guarantees ambiguity, its multiple personae of a single narrator, its consistent ambivalence, *Dog Years* is a complex novel. But as Grass's political commitment becomes more overt, his purpose in fact becomes more obvious than in *The Tin Drum*. The blurb for *Dog Years* that calls Grass "a born storyteller" is not incorrect, but he is much more than that. He is a polemical storyteller, an admonitory storyteller, an apocalyptic storyteller, and, increasingly—and fundamental to the other storytellers—a political storyteller. As such, he allows Eddi Amsel and Walter Matern, his heroes of the 1961 novel, *Dog Years,* to survive the Nazi apocalypse, the former in prosperity and good health, the latter perhaps not quite so auspiciously, while in *The Tin Drum* Oskar Matzerath is a problematic survivor unlikely to enjoy much of either health or prosperity.

The more overt political underlay of *Dog Years,*[1] with its ambivalent accommodation and rebirth, seems to coincide with the increasing political awareness and activity of Günter Grass. To be sure, one should not regard him as a political tyro before 1961, for his first encounter with Social Democratic politics occurred in spring 1947, his involvement grew during the succeeding decade,[2] and is amply reflected in *The Tin Drum.* But Grass assigns his fundamental decision to be active in *both* the literary and political spheres to 1961, and the first section of the collection of his political essays and speeches bears the subtitle "Political Beginnings: 1961,[3] that is to say, contemporaneously with the publication of *Dog Years.*

# 5

## Political Speeches and Writings

Grass's second career in politics, reflected in numerous addresses, essays, open letters, and polemics, was based consistently on advocacy of both causes and candidates, but never on his own candidacy, or even his availability, for political office. Avoiding the designation "politician" in its usual opprobrious sense, one notes that in his political writings as in his political activities Grass shows a development from idealistic amateurism to pragmatism, followed, finally, by a tempering of active involvement.

In pursuing this second track of his two-tracked career, Grass is essentially a trailblazer. The German tradition has been to separate and compartmentalize intellect and power in a rigid manner. Accordingly a career as a writer or artist effectively precluded even dabbling in, let alone actively pursuing, politics. There have been partial exceptions: Heinrich Heine's quixotic social advocacy; Goethe's career in the grand ducal establishment in Weimar long before the emergence of democracy in Germany; Thomas Mann's uncomfortable role in exile politics after the violent disappearance of democracy in Germany. Mann's much earlier *Reflections of a Nonpolitical Man* represents the more traditional distinction of roles. Günter Grass has been the latter-day pioneer in breaking the taboo, in reducing if not leveling the conceptual barrier. Not surprisingly, in doing so he has provided a prominent target for critics on both sides of the lowered barrier—literary critics as well as political critics.

Like his poetry, and unlike his fiction, Grass's political writings are only partially available in English. Still, a reading of what is available will yield rich rewards for the reader of English in an increased understanding and enjoyment of the fiction. In Grass's case, the one genre implies the other, and of course, in Grass fashion, the implication may run in either direction. To be a writer, Grass says, is to be an engaged writer. His engagement in both senses is an unabashed political love affair with democracy. It is a demanding, sometimes exhausting affair, but like Walt Whitman, whom he frequently quotes, his constant song is to democracy: "Of thee I sing!" Subsequently he modifies democracy to "evolutionary democracy."

Grass's self-proclaimed political bench mark of 1961 was prophetic of what was to come: in the one instance support of Willy Brandt, then mayor of West Berlin, and the Social Democratic party (SPD); in the second instance outrage at the repression practiced by the Communist dictatorship in East Berlin and East Germany. From early on Grass had no love for Konrad Adenauer, the then much-praised Chancellor of West Germany and leader of the Christian Democratic party. When Adenauer, who led an avowedly Christian political party, permitted himself invidious references to Willy Brandt's bastard origins, a furious Grass lent his writing and editing talents to behind-the-scenes work in behalf of Brandt and the Social Democrats. In the second, anti-Communist category of his political interest, Grass sent an open letter to the aged German Jewish poetess Anna Seghers, living in East Berlin, who, he notes, had "formed" him and his perceptions when he was a child. In the letter he implores her to exert her influence in a denunciation of the "concentration camp" that is East Germany. The problem here is one that Grass confronts by analogy later, in 1979, in

*The Meeting at Telgte:* in the latter, no one in power would in any case pay attention to the assembled writers' peace manifesto. In 1961 no one in East Germany would have paid any attention to Anna Seghers, even if with her international reputation giving her some leeway, she had dared to speak up.

Grass's third bit of political involvement in 1961 consisted of a rather whimsical and self-conscious public appeal to vote for the SPD. The appeal was his contribution to a pocket book edited by Martin Walser under the title, *The Alternative, or Do We Need a New Government?* (In later years Grass fell out with Martin Walser, whose increasingly sharp turns to the left became too much for him.) The "Government" in Walser's title is that of Adenauer, whom of course Grass attacks sharply. But the little essay is more interesting for its revelations of Grass, the literary writer, as a political novice. It is laced with personal and personal-literary references, some of the latter almost too coyly clever. For example: "Not that I'm claiming that Oskar Matzerath votes SPD."

In 1965 Grass took part in the parliamentary election campaign on the broadest possible front. As he notes with effect: fifty-two cities, fifty-two speeches. He is still a free-lancer, however, still looked at with as much reserve as gratitude by the SPD organization. After all, their famous supporter was also in many eyes infamous as a blasphemous and pornographic author. (Just being an author, breaking the taboo against politicking, would have been bad enough.) And the writer inside the political activist is still clearly evident in his use of anecdotes, his allusions, and his difficulty in getting down to the nitty-gritty characterizing operational politics. Still, in a speech conceived during a visit to the Eastern Shore of Maryland, he renounces the temptation to daring metaphors—to use his own phrase— suggested by the empty beer cans on the beach, because of his concern for the plight of Germany. One may suggest that the metaphors would concern American conspicuous consumption. Having turned his thoughts to his own country, Grass somewhat elliptically proceeds to state his position in favor of reducing the voting age (the impropriety of denying the vote to eighteen-year-olds, who after all are old enough to serve in the military). Further, he rejects as unconstitutional the provision by which a German political party must have previously obtained 5 percent of the vote in order to qualify for participation in parliamentary elections. Toward the beginning of this speech, "The Issue," delivered in the summer of 1965, Grass is still quoting from Walt Whitman. But toward the end he denounces in plain terms Adenauer's reluctantly anointed successor, Ludwig Erhard, and lauds Erhard's opponent, Willy Brandt, and the Social Democrats. Then, as if not entirely comfortable with plain advocacy, he reverts to Whitman.

Political critics were not slow to denounce "the tin drummer," as they called the literary invader, on the grounds and in the manner that Grass surely knew they would. He continued doggedly, fazed but not defeated by criticism and hisses. One of his more memorable speeches from that same summer is his "Song in Praise of Willy," in which his resentment at the savaging of Brandt finds eloquent and ironic expression. Once again Grass begins with a citation from Walt Whitman, in this case Whitman singing the praises of the murdered Lincoln: "O powerful western fallen star!" Grass proposes, on the other hand, "to sing the praises of a living man: Willy Brandt"—a defamed living man, he might perhaps have pointed out.

In his praise of Brandt, Grass touches especially on two points that hold lasting significance for Grass, and that within a few years emerge interrelatedly in his life and his literature in a most ironic way. First, he declares that if the professional politicians and the political establishment of the SPD continue lukewarm toward Brandt and continue to play safe, traditional politics, they will continue to drive the most gifted youthful members out of the party and into the arms of splinter leftist groups. Second, referring to the workers' uprising in East Berlin on June 17, 1953, he maintains that Brandt was the first person to protest the falsification of that uprising into a national revolt.

That workers' uprising in East Berlin, and Bert Brecht's refusal to support it, comprise the thematic basis of Grass's play, *The Plebeians Rehearse the Uprising,* which he was trying to write in the same year he campaigned for Brandt. As to Grass's early perception of the disaffection of youth with the SPD and youth's consequent desertion, radicalization, and protest, it proved all too accurate an indicator of what was to come, although perhaps he could not yet foresee that it would come home to roost with him as an early advocate and intercessor for youth in such a painful and ironic way. The student protest movement snowballed. Already in 1967 an invasion of radical students was a factor in the disbandment of Group 47. In 1969 Grass published *Local Anaesthetic* and premiered *Max: A Play,* in both of which he finds the student radicals to be somewhat self-indulgent and in any case pursuing completely ineffective methods to effect reform. Of course they denounced him, probably in most cases not even aware that he had pleaded their cause at its very inception.

On September 19, 1965, the Christian Democratic party won the parliamentary election; the SPD lost. Three weeks later Grass received the Georg Büchner Prize, named for Georg Büchner (1813-1837), dramatist (*The Death of Danton* and *Woyzeck,* both often still performed) and revolutionary, who died in exile in Zurich. Instead of a polite acceptance speech, Grass delivered "to an audience of the defeated" a bitter assessment of the campaign conducted by the SPD, as well as of the condition of West Germany, not forgetting in the process his own fifty-two speeches on the road to defeat. This speech is entitled "On the Self-Evident," which in the German original becomes the title of the first collection of Grass's speeches and essays to be published as a book. Grass is tired of anecdote, tired of his opponents' slanders. He attacks what he calls the "national bankruptcy" of West Germany and "the platitude-spewing conscience of a nonexistent nation." As for the "economic miracle," Grass in his disdain of the consumer society notes that "the dance around the Golden Calf can go on for another four years."

Never a friend of German academia, Grass assigns a major share of the blame for political defeat to intellectuals in their ivory towers expatiating on abstract issues. No doubt thinking of his own work in the political trenches, he denounces what he calls "seminar Marxism," which is more interested in undoing the misery in Vietnam and Iran than in contending with the stench rising from domestic politics and more interested in composing an "interminable epic hymn to Fidel Castro" than making "a simple plea for Willy Brandt." He himself is coming closer and closer to being a predominantly practical politician rather than a writer engaging in politics—which doesn't say that he is not eloquently familiar with Georg Büchner, his equally unorthodox predecessor.

In fact it takes just one more disillusionment in the grubby arena of politics to make Günter Grass abandon his last remaining literary illusions about politics. That disillusionment was the so-called Great Coalition, entered into on December 1, 1966, by which the Christian Democrats and the SPD joined in the governance of the country. Willy Brandt accepted the vice-chancellorship. Kurt Georg Kiesinger, who had been a Nazi from 1933 to 1945, became Chancellor. Grass, still adhering to the not necessarily literary notion that politics could be made consonant with morality, was aghast. He attacked on several fronts, not excepting the SPD itself, whose principles seemed to him severely compromised if not indeed bartered.

He immediately dispatched an open letter to Willy Brandt, in which he again raised the all too ominous matter of the desertion of the young from the SPD. He directed another open letter to Kiesinger, imploring him not to accept the chancellorship. But while Grass was correct in assessing the importance of the youthful exodus from the SPD and from parliamentary politics as a whole, events were to prove that neither the Great Coalition nor the neo-Nazi party had seriously damaged the West German state. Grass continued to attack Kiesinger frontally and unremittingly in both literature and speeches . In "The Pinprick Speech" of January 29, 1967, Grass asks pointedly, "Can a Nazi become Chancellor?" The embittered reply: "If he has repented, yes, certainly."

At the death of Konrad Adenauer, Grass wrote an "Obituary of an Opponent" that contains a few charitable lines but is in general unforgiving. Later in 1967 Grass took on the monolithic Springer press, publisher of newspapers and picture journalism. Springer had suggested by apparently faked reports that all was not well between the East German writer Arnold Zweig and the East German government. A lie, declares Grass, springing to the aid of his colleague on the other side of the Wall, a lie calculated to make trouble for Zweig, who lives in the East because he prefers to.

Grass was no ideological friend of Zweig, nor of the militant student leader Rudi Dutschke, called "Red Rudi" in the American press. Yet after an attempt on Dutschke's life, incited, according to Grass, by the Springer press, Grass deplores the violence and the counterviolence. None of it helps anything, for it is emotional and lacks any political content. He finds the same speech, given on May 1, 1968, a suitable occasion to denounce not only the colonels' dictatorship in Greece, but NATO, and the American use of napalm in Vietnam.

In 1969 Grass, fervently dedicated to ending the Great Coalition, again played an energetic role in the parliamentary elections. This time his approach is distinctly more pragmatic. His appearances—approximately ninety of them—were officially sponsored and supported by the SPD. And this time his speeches are almost purely political, inspirational only on a political basis. At this point Grass seems to be a practicing, realistic politician. The SPD wins, and Willy

Brandt, still his friend, becomes Chancellor.

In late October 1969 Grass delivered a lecture at a writers' congress in Belgrade, Yugoslavia, entitled "Literature and Revolution, or the Idylist's Snorting Hobby-Horse." If the title is fanciful, the first sentence of the speech is plain: "To begin with, I am an opponent of revolution." He goes on to declare his aversion to "the absolute demands, the inhumane intolerance" of revolution. Revolution is not a historical necessity and it will always find its reward in permanent counterrevolution. He declares himself a revisionist or, "even worse," a social democrat. The mechanism of revolution is the same whether the revolution is of the left or of the right. Even the role of literature suborned by revolution is of the same pattern, whether left or right: Brecht's hymns to Stalin are not essentially different from the philosopher Martin Heidegger's obeisances to the Nazis. For his international literary colleagues in Belgrade, Grass makes use of plentiful literary references and insights. In his Belgrade address one can see a harbinger of his celebrated "return to literature," which presumably began slightly more than two years later with preliminary work on *The Flounder*. It may be questioned whether the rise of the political man necessarily has to coincide with an eclipse of the writer. For already in a May Day speech of 1970, given in Baden-Baden, Grass is picturesquely employing the basic metaphor of *From the Diary of a Snail,* published in 1972.

The title of the 1970 May Day Speech, "The Additional Significance of Erfurt," refers to the city of Erfurt as the site of a most important SPD conference in 1891, one year after the repeal of Chancellor Otto von Bismarck's anti-Socialist laws. The program laid out by the SPD in Erfurt in 1891 gave rise, Grass elucidates, to the two strands of socialism visible to this day, the theoretical and the practical, eventually Communism and revisionism. The former, in replacing private capitalism with state capitalism to the detriment of democratic rights, merely replaces an old form of repression with a new form. Such a giant leap flies against effective if gradual reform of the system of private capitalism. To be sure, reform is snaillike, and, Grass reminds us, "there are no jumping snails."

On March 23, 1971, in the role of political organizer and adviser, Grass gave an address before the SPD parliamentary delegation. He pointed out the urgency of educational reform, environmental reform, and tax reform. His May Day 1971 address, "The Worker and His Environment," was delivered to a labor union audience in Hamburg. His primary concern in this speech is environmental resources and their protection, or lack thereof, and Willy Brandt's lack of openness on the subject.

In 1972 Grass again took to the political stump for Brandt and the SPD. Brandt was returned as Chancellor. In March 1973 Grass announced in a speech that he regarded his own political work as completed and that he proposed to withdraw from the front ranks. He had never entertained any ambition to hold office himself because he was and is content in his own profession, which he describes as "being a writer and remaining an illustrator." And, with occasional exceptions, his emphatically dual role ended. He worked on *The Flounder*. By his own account, his departure from active politics was accelerated by Willy Brandt's resignation in 1974 as a consequence of the Günter Guillaume espionage affair. Grass's participation in the 1976 election campaign was minimal. He thereafter criticized the SPD chancellor, Helmut Schmidt, for pursuing the politics of accommodation. Most recently, in concert with other writers and as an individual author of an open letter to members of the Bundestag, he has denounced the positioning of American Pershing II and cruise missiles in West Germany.

# 6

## *Local Anaesthetic/Max: A Play*

In the novel, *Local Anaesthetic* (1969), Grass departs from the locale of the Danzig Trilogy as well as from the free-flowing exuberance that characterized its three constituents. To be sure, *Local Anaesthetic* contains internal references to people and places in the earlier fiction. Indeed, the chief character in the new novel, the forty-year-old Eberhard Starusch, is the Störtebeker who at seventeen had been the leader of The Dusters youth gang. But in the way that twenty-three years have elapsed for the fictive, formerly reckless Störtebeker, some ten to twelve years have elapsed for the writer Günter Grass, during which he had become deeply committed politically. As if that alone did not inevitably affect Grass's fictional stance, now—in the late 1960s, after he had begun writing *Local Anaesthetic*—he was witness to the emergence of the new left, whose youthful apostles regarded him balefully and denounced him— employing the Maoist equation—as an anachronistic traitor-liberal.

In addition to locale and tone *Local Anaesthetic* differs also from its predecessors in dispensing with the narrative framework that has a fictive first-person narrator explaining how he came to write the work. The teacher Eberhard Starusch, having in the spring of 1967 completed a two-year treatment for overbite and an assortment of other dental woes, recounts to his dentist his experiences during that trying period. These narrated experiences include not only his actual interaction with his dentist but also his imagined interaction with his dentist *and* with his own past. Finally they include his own ongoing interactions with Philipp Scherbaum and Veronika Lewand, two seventeen-year-old students, and with Irmgard Seifert, his female colleague.

These four are the "real" persons with whom Starusch deals, although in the case of the dentist the majority of the interaction that goes beyond matters of dental treatment is evidently a product of Starusch's imagination. (At the same time there are few clues to the exact distinction between real and imaginary; dental treatment and amelioration of pain as the central thematic metaphor serves to blur the distinction further.) In addition to the "real persons," there is in Starusch's memory a cast of fanciful persons. Chief among them is Sieglinde (Linde) Krings, his supposed former fiancée; her father, the former General Krings, only now returned home after long years of Russian internment; and Heinz Schlottau, Starusch's successor in Sieglinde's affections. Starusch also conducts imaginary conversations with his long-dead mother.

There is an obvious connection and sympathy between the forty-year-old teacher, Starusch, continually adverting to his exploits as the seventeen-year-old Störtebeker, and the now seventeen-year-old student Philipp Scherbaum, called Flip (who, however, rejects Starusch's tales of youth). Similarly there is a rapport between the thirty-nine-year-old teacher, Irmgard Seifert, who at seventeen was an enthusiastic leader in the Hitler organization for girls, and the now seventeen-year-old Veronika Lewand, called Vero, enthusiastic member of the new left. And as there is a not entirely satisfying emotional and sexual relationship between Starusch and Seifert, so there is a less than satisfactory emotional and sexual relationship between Flip and Vero. The relationship between Starusch and Seifert is clouded by inhibition, the past, and Seifert's guilty feelings about her Nazi past. The relationship between Scherbaum and Lewand is clouded by the latter's uncritical espousal of Maoist doctrine.

*Local Anaesthetic* is divided into thirds of unequal length, each with its predominant although not exclusive thematic focus. In the first part Starusch is receiving treatment for his lower jaw. The prolonged treatment occasionally results in pain, made bearable by the application of local anaesthetic and by the use of a television screen to divert the patient. Regular television programming, complete with commercials, is to be seen on the screen, but Starusch's fertile imagination puts on his own programs as well. In the first section of the novel Starusch is trying to come to terms with his past, which is the basis for his flights of fancy. Although Starusch's fantasies are amenable to no dogmatic mode of interpretation, the traumatic medical intervention in his jaw is the mechanism that has triggered his fantasies of his past.

Accompanied in the first section of the novel by revelation of his present personal and professional life, these fantasies are interspersed with long discourses with the dentist. The dentist quickly emerges as an empirical scientist confident of step-by-step amelioration of pain—that is, of the human condition. He is also an adept philosopher. He knows and admires Seneca, the Roman Stoic philosopher and dramatist (4? B.C.-A.D. 65). He and Starusch use Seneca's Stoic aphorisms almost as passwords to each other's thoughts. The dentist borrows Marxist terminology and describes his plan for worldwide medicare, based on his scientific perception that everybody is, was, and will be sick, and die. He envisions a world run by and for the ill, because there are no longer any healthy people, nor is there any compulsion to be healthy. Starusch worries about how this grandiose scheme would comport with his own dream of the world as a pedagogical province in which everyone learns and no one teaches.

Those critics who would make Starusch Grass's sole authorial representative in the novel err in the corresponding tendency to interpret the dentist as a narrow-minded technocrat.[1] Far from it. The dentist is Grass's representative too—the part of him that has come to see that there can be no grand reform of the world; that you bridge over what exists, say disease or malformation, without counting on extirpation; that you do what you can in your own corner. If the dentist's faith in science as a limited agent of amelioration is almost too naive, unlimited faith in man is no better.

A rigid critical polarization of Starusch and his dentist overlooks the fact that much of the nondental discourse presumably between Starusch and his dentist is really between Starusch and Starusch. What "taciturn" dentist involves himself so verbosely in the emotional and psychological life of his patient? The figure of the dentist might better be imagined as the means or the model by which Starusch works through his problematic past, then through his hardly less problematic present to something like a synthesis—a practical and humane understanding. The parallel between Starusch's need for some such synthesis and Germany's need, as seen by Grass, is obvious.

Starusch's "real" past seems to include, with some allowance for uncertainty: his experiences as Störtebeker, leader of a youth gang in Danzig; capture and impressed military service in the last years of World War II, including landmine clearing without protective firecover; on-the-job training, perhaps as a work-study student, with a cement company that had grown from a stonecutting enterprise; and an engagement, painfully broken, with an unnamed girl.

Starusch's fantasy-past is richer, or at any rate is adumbrated in much richer detail. He is supposedly a resourceful and inventive engineer in the cement industry, concerned above all with processes to reclaim economically and profitably the cement dust that pollutes the area. Employed by a giant Krings cement company, he is engaged to marry the daughter of the family, Linde, and his fantastic reconstruction does not neglect the sexual aspect of their relationship. The founder and long-absent owner of the cement company, General Ferdinand Krings, returns from ten years of Russian captivity. (The prototype of Krings is Field Marshal Ferdinand Schörner, who was appointed commander-in-chief of the German army during Hitler's final days. Schörner stood trial in West Germany for executing soldiers without benefit of courtmartial. He received a four-and-a-half-year sentence. When Grass wrote his novel, Schörner was living comfortably in Munich.)

Starusch loses his imagined fiancée, Linde Krings, to the wiles of the electrician Heinz Schlottau, who as an enlisted man had accompanied Krings on his campaigns. General Krings is obsessed with refighting all the lost battles on the German-Russian front of World War II, resorting to elaborate sandbox restaging of the lost battles (the working title of the novel), that with hindsight can become victorious battles won by Krings. Krings's endeavors, as fantasized by Starusch, seem to correspond logically with, first, Starusch's bouts of nostalgia for the lost arena of his youth, that is, Danzig, the East; and second, with postwar efforts (as, for example, proposed by Günter Grass) to effect political reunion of some sort with the lost—from the West German standpoint—territories of the East.

Some of the more spectacular scenes that Starusch sees on the dentist's television screen are composed of bulldozers attacking mountains of consumer products: cosmetics, camping equipment, home movie projectors, ready-made products of every kind. Here the reader sees, quite literally, a reflection of Grass's conviction that West Germany's infatuation with consumer goods is prejudicial to the more urgent political business of coming to grips with its Nazi past and with former Nazis in high places both in business—the fictive Ferdinand Krings—and government—the all too real Chancellor of the Republic, Kurt Georg Kiesinger, called "Silver-Tongue."

During Starusch's conversations with the dentist in the

first section of the novel the students, Philipp Scherbaum
and Veronika Lewand, are merely sketched in. In the second
section, a respite in dental treatment but hardly a pause in
Starusch's conversations with the dentist, Flip and Vero
move from the background to the foreground. Flip, bright
and sensitive, is outraged by the course of the American war
in Vietnam with, as he sees it, the injustice and cruelty and
death visited wantonly on the Vietnamese. He symbolizes all
this under the heading of napalm. Flip's outrage at politics
in West Germany and at inhumanity in Vietnam is so
overwhelming that he rejects as less than meaningless the
possibility of becoming editor of the school paper and of
campaigning from this forum, in response to heated student
demand, for a designated smoking area on the school
grounds.

Vero Lewand, Flip's girlfriend, is obsessed by new left
revolutionism, which she embraces without any semblance
of critical thought. She quotes tiresomely the jargon and the
slogans, she loves being a member of the group, and going to
their parties. She seems to be devoted to her boyfriend, but
in fact she is more devoted to trying to bring him into
alignment with her own naive revolutionary zeal, to
persuading him to act rather than think, to separating him
from the restraining, discursive influence of Starusch.

Vero exerts the full force of her influence on Flip after the
latter decides, in moral outrage and deep anger at the events
in Vietnam, to immolate his beloved dachshund Max as a
public spectacle in full view of the middle-class women
stuffing themselves with pastry on the balcony of the Hotel
Kempinski. Why a dog? the dentist wonders, when Starusch
tells him of Flip's resolve to act. Because, Starusch tells him,
Berliners are notorious for their affection for dogs. Flip will
use gasoline on Max in place of napalm. There will be an
explanatory sign. The members of the consuming society
will look up from their self-indulgence to take notice of a
dog burning—more readily, in fact, than if it were a person
being burned, or Jesus Christ being crucified. "Do it, Flip

come on, do it," Vero keeps urging.

Starusch devises tactics to forestall Flip's action, which is not only inhumane but ineffective in ending the tragic misery in Vietnam. Starusch notes that public burnings satisfy a desire more than they excite a repulsion. He offers historical analogies complete with color slides, he gives philosophical and literary rationales against the action. He urges Flip to sublimate his anger in protest songs. He even threatens to report Flip to the police. Finally, if the deed must be done, he suggests that it be some dog other than Max, perhaps a dog from an animal shelter. Flip sticks to his guns, encouraged by Vero not to fall for the typical liberal gambit of instituting dialogue to deter action.

Starusch visits Flip at the latter's home. On the wall he notices a picture of someone in the garb of his own generation. It is Scherbaum's hero, Helmuth Hübener, who as a member of an undercover group had disseminated transcripts of forbidden British news broadcasts about the war. Hübener, after being tortured, was executed at Plötzensee prison in 1942. How old was Kurt Georg Kiesinger, now Chancellor, in 1942? Flip asks. Kiesinger, replies Starusch, joined the Nazis in 1933 at the age of twenty-nine. Flip explodes with loathing and outrage. He is more than ever resolved to proceed with the immolation of Max in protest not only against the Americans in Vietnam but against a system that permits a Kiesinger to become federal Chancellor.

Starusch, his resources of dissuasion apparently exhausted (and having been seduced by Vero in her effort to get him off Flip's case), sets up an appointment between the dentist and Flip. The initially professional relationship, which the dentist can rationalize because Flip has dental problems too, deepens into a personal relationship that includes discussion of the pros and cons of Flip's plan. Flip actually abandons his plan. But not, as the dentist believes, owing to *his* expertness in discussion.

Rather the abandonment is the result of a collision

between theory and practice as it affects Flip emotionally. He and Starusch reconnoiter the locale of the proposed dog-burning. At the scene Flip involuntarily anticipates the spectators by vomiting violently. If not completely dissuaded by his own reaction, he now has misgivings, reinforced by a future vision of himself at forty, Starusch's age, "peddling the feats of a seventeen-year-old," as Starusch does with his tales of his exploits as the youthful gang leader. Vero and Irmgard Seifert have failed in their incitement of Flip. Action has been forestalled, if not entirely by discourse, then to a degree by Flip's own personality. It would be stretching the fictional facts to say that he has perceived intellectually the fact that burning a dog in Berlin is not likely to contribute either to peace in Vietnam or the the replacement of the federal Chancellor. But the result is the same. Flip becomes a gradual reformist in the mold of his mentor Starusch—and of Günter Grass. In an interview touching on *Local Anaesthetic,* Grass dialectically assures us that by taking a skeptical position—born of the experience of his own generation—toward violence, he could at the peak moment of the euphoria of violence see and anticipate the resignative relapse. Flip, lacking that experience, and Starusch, can arrive at perception only by an emotional shortcut.[2]

Coincident with the third section of the novel, Starusch's dental treatment resumes: he must now undergo intervention in his upper jaw. His fantasies of his past resume. As for Flip, his first article as editor of the school newspaper is denied print. It is on "Silver-Tongue," Kurt Georg Kiesinger, the former Nazi and present Chancellor. On the other hand, Flip's editorial campaign for a smoking area—he is a passionate nonsmoker himself—meets with success, "A small success." commends Starusch, reflecting with inevitable irony his own doctrine of progress.

Supposedly as the result of a bit of personal investigation of the scene, the dentist undermines Starusch's fanciful stories of his past. Fantasy is certified as fantasy, but that does not end the fantasizing. Starusch, after belatedly achieving a relatively satisfactory sexual relationship with Irmgard Seifert, becomes engaged to her. They do not marry, nor do they break the engagement. Two years later they are still engaged. By that time Vero Lewand, leaving school just before her examinations, has married a Canadian linguist. Philipp Scherbaum is studying medicine. And Eberhard Starusch suffers from a deep infection in his lower jaw. His bridge, the dentist's pride and joy, has to be sawn through. Nothing lasts. There are always new sources of pain to be endured—with the help, one infers, of local anaesthetic.

*Local Anaesthetic* contains a twofold moral. First, doubtless the one Grass started with, is that the present is irrevocably conditioned by the past: what comes afterward is already contained in what comes before, to paraphrase Grass. In fact, the drama version of *Local Anaesthetic* bears the German title *Davor,* literally "before." In the context of the novel and the play, the "before" is Nazism, the totalitarianism of the radical right, the only radicalism that Grass had so far experienced at first hand. (Of course he had bruised the official intellectual left with *The Plebeians Rehearse the Uprising* three years earlier.) The "after" correlative with the "before" is post-World War II West Germany, the Federal Republic, hospitable to former Nazis, always threatened, in Grass's view, by the possibility of reverting to right-wing totalitarianism, continually reluctant to deal with its past in the nirvana of consumption. The Social Democratic party, for which he had campaigned, had entered into a coalition with the center party, led by former Nazi Kiesinger. And a new right—all too reminiscent of the old right—was regrouping in the wings of the political stage. "Lost Battles," the working title of the novel, probably reflected with accuracy Grass's perception of the fate of liberal democracy in Germany.

The second moral of *Local Anaesthetic,* which seems to be superimposed on the original one, is that the only effective mode of change is not thoughtless revolutionary

violence but rather reform that proceeds rationally and
thoughtfully. One is advised to forget grand and showy and
violent revolutionary programs committed to absolutes,
because they are not only inhumane but ineffective. This
would seem to be Grass's response to the zealots of the new
left who were making headlines while he was writing his
novel—his first direct experience of the radicalism of the
left. Whatever his emotional response to the new left may
have been, on the level of practical political philosophy
Grass—a socialist, an admirer of the father of socialist
revisionism, Eduard Bernstein—could only be appalled, a
reaction strikingly reflected in *Local Anaesthetic*. The new
left in turn regarded Grass, no defender of the establishment,
in the same way that the fictive Vero Lewand regarded
Eberhard Starusch, as a traitor, a liberal.

*Max: A Play* is a dramatization of the second, the central
section of *Local Anaesthetic*. (A previous partial English
version goes under the name *Uptight*.) Grass apparently
worked on the play simultaneously with the novel, although
the publication date of the German original (1970) is a year
later. Focusing as it does on the middle part of the novel, the
play does not, on the one hand, develop or dwell upon
Starusch's past, his evidently traumatic early broken
engagement, nor, on the other hand, on his later engagement
to Irmgard Seifert or on Scherbaum's medical studies or on
Lewand's apparent abandonment of Maoism in favor of the
more conventional romance of marriage.

What is left is a dramatic discourse—with the emphasis on
the noun—on Flip's dilemma: shall he carry out his resolve
to burn Max in protest, or shall he desist? As we already
know, the discussion is fatal to the action (if not Max);
nothing happens. There are five participants in a continuing
round of variously configured discussion groups: Scherbaum,
Starusch, Lewand, Seifert, and the dentist. The last functions
not only narratively but also structurally as a moderator or a
conductor.

The play is divided into thirteen scenes, each flowing

smoothly into another. The stage is open, with but the barest of props (such as the dentist's chair). The actors come and go, Flip and Vero most often by means of bicycles. Schematic pairing is more concentrated than in the novel. That is, the students seem to represent more of an entity in attacking the teachers, who are themselves more united. But no entity and no individual represents an immutable point of view. Each has his or her strong points and weak points of argument. But as they discuss, it becomes increasingly evident that Flip will in the end not take the action he had once felt compelled to take.

We are reminded of Grass's earlier poetic dramas, in which the dramatic conflict, such as it was, consisted in the absence or negation of conflict. Seneca the Stoic is enlisted parodistically; his precepts contribute to the abortion of action. In the end Flip has taken over the editorship of the school newspaper. Vero, still exhorting to action, boycotts Flip's editorial conference. The ultimate boycott is an ultimate ironic emphasis, for the provocateur Vero applies nonaction, and the play ends.

Inevitably one compares *Local Anaesthetic* with *Max: A Play,* probably to the disadvantage of the play, which lacks dramatic conflict or development. The play naturally cannot reproduce the full scope of the novel. Grass had to take that portion of the novel offering the potentially greatest dramatic conflict around which to build his play. But that conflict proves inadequate for theater; it is a play that very much resembles his early plays. It is demonstrated once again that while imagistic theater is aesthetically enjoyable, it cannot entirely compensate for the absence of dramatic action.

The novel itself found a critical reception distinctly cooler than that accorded to *The Tin Drum* and *Cat and Mouse.* For one thing, *Local Anaesthetic* follows the precedent of the third member of the Trilogy, *Dog Years,* in exploring the possibilities of bolder, less linear narrative structure—in this respect anticipating at least in a general way the structure of Grass's later fiction. It may be, however, that with *Local Anaesthetic* the flashback technique, formerly eschewed by Grass, has been used to excess—however much it seems the ideal narrative avenue by which to connect politics, present and (inseparably) past, with a highly developed and extended parable in the present.

# 7.

## *From the Diary of a Snail*

Although the title of *From the Diary of a Snail* (1972) may suggest otherwise, the work is more novel than diary. The structure is not at all loose and whimsical, as is perhaps typical of literary diaries. Even less is the book a monologue. Indeed, as Grass in the role of pedagogue narrates his twofold, interwoven didactic novel to his four children (ranging in age from four to eleven), *From the Diary of a Snail* emerges as his most precisely and subtly organized prose work since *The Tin Drum*.

Grass's sketch on the book jacket is protean in its implications. One needs to look at the entire jacket, not just the front panel. The half-profile of a somewhat frozen-looking human face of larger than natural size, expansively and predominantly white, lies horizontally against a sharply delineated, arbitrary horizon of blue. On the forehead, crawling onto the nose, is a snail, brilliant orange in color. Its face is turned toward a mirror-image snail in black and white lying on the horizon line. The only bit of color in the human face is a wide-open eye of blue-green, focusing in the direction of the warm-colored snail.

The face lies beneath the plane marked by the horizon line. One may be inclined to relate that "subterranean" (or perhaps underwater) location to the marked prominence of subterranean locales—for example, basements—in Grass's fiction. In *From the Diary of a Snail* the chief locale will be the basement in which Hermann Ott takes refuge from the Nazis and—collects snails. It may be that the human eye in the sketch reflects a certain terror, not, I would think, of the beneficent snail, but of what the world is like outside the low-lying refuge. The snail is positive, warm in color (though its foot is doubtless cool and sticky). The snail within the novel will be the means of eliminating—even over-eliminating—the melancholic affliction of Lisbeth Stomma and of causing her to become, at last, emotionally and physically responsive to Ott's lovemaking. In this vein one may have noted the vagina-like outline of the eye as sketched. The snail, whatever one's mistakenly fastidious misgivings about it, proves to be Grass's ideal agent of progress, and not only erotic progress. Grass would even use the snail instead of the rooster as the symbol of the Social Democratic party.

As *From the Diary of a Snail* resembles *The Tin Drum* in its elegant arrangement of different but thematically connected time periods, the new novel portends its successors in what has become a hallmark of Grass's fiction: the narrator, as Günter Grass, plays an important role in the novel, not only in recounting autobiographical details, but also in visibly directing the fictional traffic. Autobiographical and fictional: those are two interwoven and counterpointed narrations in the *Diary*. In the first the author narrates his own adventures and misadventures as a political campaigner for the Social Democratic party in the West German parliamentary elections of 1969. In the second he draws on his boyhood memories of Danzig in the 1930s before and during the Nazi terror to narrate a fiction about Hermann Ott, teacher of German and biology, nicknamed Doubt (and without doubt a persona of Grass himself, already on record as an advocate of healthy doubt).

These two disparate strands of narration are drawn together for the benefit of his children and, as Grass specifies, other people's children as well, to the end that they avoid the temptation of political absolutism whether of the right or the left. Further, as proof against the promises of the absolutists, he warns children to be alert to and renounce the political quick fix of utopia. Progress can only come slowly. The model of progress is the snail, owing to its slow, steady, indefatigable pursuit of its goal, as well as to its absorptive powers. In this absorptive role the snail is capable, at least in the Danzig fiction, of mediating between utopia and melancholy, which are symbiotic: the former cannot exist without the balancing constraint of the latter, and vice versa.

Grass makes the story of Hermann Ott the symbol of the crimes of the Nazis against the Jews of Danzig. This role assignment of Hermann Ott has its irony as well as its sorrow, for Ott is not a Jew at all. But by teaching in the Jewish school, by maintaining friendships with Jews after it became unwise to do so, he finds himself obliged to go underground soon after the outbreak of World War II, marked by the German invasion of Poland. In preparation for going underground, Ott, called Doubt, has to repatriate to their various habitats the snails comprising the collection that was his pride and joy.

Doubt, the literate and atheistic non-Jewish German, takes refuge with an illiterate Kashubian who finds it to his advantage to obtain official classification as a German. Anton Stomma, who needs assistance in filling out his application for Germanization, proves the safest host possible for Doubt (whom, because of his learnedness, Stomma takes to be a Jew). Stomma runs a bicycle repair shop in conjunction with a subsistence farm. He has few social contacts. He lives alone with his twenty-three-year-old daughter Lisbeth. Lisbeth was nineteen when her lover, a Pole, was killed on the fourth day of the war. On the first day of the war their three-year-old son was run over and killed by a military vehicle. Thrown into an autistic depression by these losses, Lisbeth becomes mute; her only contacts are with the dead in graveyards. Stomma's is an ideal refuge for

Doubt because it has a well-situated basement, right under the kitchen, with which it is connected by a trap door. Doubt agrees to pay Stomma three marks a day. (His money runs out at the time of the German defeat at Stalingrad in November 1942; but Stomma does not evict him.)

Doubt teaches Stomma to write—to fill out the Germanization forms—but not to read. That omission reserves to Doubt the function of reading to his host from the daily newspaper, which helps secure Doubt's tenure in the Stomma basement a bit more firmly. Not that Stomma ever seriously considers evicting Doubt. A free spirit, he prides himself on having a "Jew" in his basement, perhaps especially as German military power wanes. The basement becomes a cultural arena. Doubt reads Aesop's fables to Anton and Lisbeth Stomma, then invents original fables. Changing character by changing hats, Doubt enacts simplified versions of the German classics for his hosts, not omitting the opportunity to parody German militarism. Doubt's debunking of heroism, however, proves uncomfortably disillusioning to Stomma, who, as German arms falter, has imagined himself in the glorious role of liberator of Kashubia. Deprived of such glory, Stomma subjects Doubt to a beating with his leather belt. Despite the beatings, it is a rather convivial, if limited existence among the bicycle parts and the spartan sleeping accommodations—a mattress on the floor—in Stomma's basement.

Three months after the turning point of Stalingrad, Stomma begins sending Lisbeth to the basement to lie down on the mattress and make herself sexually available to Doubt. Obedient and dutiful, she does so without complaint, but also without the slightest flicker of reciprocal enjoyment or passion. Her mind, detached from present reality, is in the graveyard. She is incapable of sexual response. For Doubt, lovemaking in such a circumstance is nonetheless, at least at first, a pleasant habit. But eventually frustration at Lisbeth's complete unresponsiveness balances out his physical satisfaction.

In March 1943, with the fortune of German arms still declining, a snail is by chance brought into the basement by Lisbeth, apparently with some potatoes. Doubt is enchanted, to the point of both laughing and crying, at the reunion with the object of his former collector's affection. Perhaps Lisbeth divined his wish. She next begins gathering and bringing to him a variety of snails and slugs that inhabit graveyards, together with foliage, rotted wood, and mossy stones to make them comfortable. Stomma adapts happily enough to the new inhabitants of his basement with the not insignificant observation that at least they won't make any noise. Spirited snail races, run under elaborate, strict, and humane conditions, become the order of the day in the subterranean refuge.

One day Lisbeth brings home a purple slug (German *Schnecke* can mean slug as well as snail) that Doubt cannot identify, even with application of the most rigorous scientific method. The new member of the snail family stimulates his doubt: where can Lisbeth have found it? It will revolutionize—therefore change to excess—her life. When Doubt puts it on her arm, on her hand and knee, she who has been mute for years begins to grunt and stammer, then to speak intelligible words. She talks out, almost in the way of psychotherapy—of which one may well see a parody—her bereavement at the loss of her son and her former lover, verbalizing her pent-up anguish.

But this therapeutic slug is much more than a mere parody of what Grass elsewhere calls a "ritual." The entire novel, as Grass has noted at the outset, is an outgrowth of a lecture that he has agreed to deliver two years later in Nuremberg in observance of the fifth centenary of the birth of the artist Albrecht Dürer. The lecture, which constitutes an epilogue to the novel, will dwell on Dürer's celebrated copperplate engraving, *Meleancolia I*. And it is melancholia that the miracle slug seems to suck out of Lisbeth. As it absorbs the black temperament that has so long afflicted her, the slug becomes violet, then blue-black. Lisbeth in turn

becomes psychologically and emotionally normal—
spectacularly so.

Doubt no longer need be frustrated in his attempts to
awaken her passion. It is Lisbeth, now insatiable, who
initiates, demands, improvises. Doubt throws himself without
restraint, or doubt, into the resultant lovemaking. Meanwhile
Lisbeth's interest in social life increases in corresponding
measure. She gossips and is hungry for gossip. As he yields
completely and thus unwisely to passion, Doubt discovers
she can be normally callous and offensive, as well as
affectionate. Lisbeth signals her full normality by getting a
permanent wave. On the first Sunday of Advent, her
increasing distaste for the redeeming slug is culminated by
her trampling it, killing her redeemer.

A normal woman with a permanent wave and a wildly
adoring lover, Lisbeth becomes a nagging mistress (as Dürer
is said to have had a nagging wife). Sure of herself, she is not
blind to the possibly exploitable vulnerability of her lover-
refugee hidden in her basement. As the German armies
continue to retreat, and the front comes closer, her threats to
report Doubt to the police become more blatant. Nor are her
threats diminished by the fact she is now pregnant. But when
the Germans leave and the area is occupied by units of the
Soviet Second Army, Doubt succeeds in protecting Lisbeth
from being raped, as well as interceding successfully in
behalf of her father, whose official German ethnicity is now
a considerable liability.

Thereafter Doubt, known again as Hermann Ott, having
married the former Lisbeth Stomma, searches graveyards
for two years for the unidentified purple slug. While he
searches, he succumbs gradually to melancholia. Lisbeth,
now the mother of a son Arthur, has Ott committed to a
mental institution, where in the course of twelve years his
muttering degenerates into muteness. This must be his
penalty for having abandoned his characteristic salutary
doubt, precisely in the area of love where, above all, no
panacea nor utopia exists. It is permissible to alleviate

melancholia, but not to eradicate it, for then there is no counterbalance to the resulting utopia, which is likewise intolerable in pure form. Melancholia and utopia are mutually supportive, not mutually exclusive.

But Hermann Ott does recover. In the late 1950s together with Lisbeth and Arthur he leaves the People's Republic of Poland—the successor regime in Danzig, or Gdańsk—and migrates to West Germany. For a while he serves as a cultural affairs official. Today—that is, in 1969—he lives in retirement with Lisbeth, occasionally giving lectures on such topics as the snail as an ancient fertility symbol.

The snail or slug is both fertility symbol and much more than that. It is a sexual symbol by virtue of its folkloristic vaginal associations. The purple miracle slug brought to the basement by Lisbeth, which Doubt repeatedly puts on her body to treat her melancholia, on November 6, 1944, induces sexual excitement culminating four minutes later in orgasm. With this her recovery is complete, and Doubt, as Grass explains, at last has a woman. The same slug is a religious symbol, a Redeemer slain. "Nail the slug to the cross," Grass interjects, in case the reader has been slow in grasping the connection. And the slug, spilling inky black fluid as it is trampled, is the symbol of Grass himself, whose medium is ink. Even more it is a symbol of Grass as a writer who, having absorbed the blackness of the society he writes about (Nazism and its remnant survival in West Germany), finds himself rejected not only by those Nazi remnants but also—to be sure, for different reasons—by the young middle-class radicals of the left.

Side by side, dovetailed significantly with the story of Doubt and his snails, Grass narrates the diary of another snail—himself—as a campaigner for the Social Democratic party in the election of 1969. It is a grueling, if rewarding experience: day after day, one town after another, hotel rooms, meetings, ninety-four speeches. And perhaps some snaillike progress. The Social Democratic vote increases by 3.4 percent; and the Social Democrats, in coalition with the

Free Democrats, are enabled to form a government. Grass does not glamorize the political drama nor the chief actors in it. He does not deny or gloss over the paradoxes or untidy aspects. But neither does he forget that democracy and its processes are on the whole superior to some recent and current alternative modes of government.

Probably the most notable real-life event during the campaign, and certainly the most shocking, is the public suicide of the pharmacist Manfred Augst, a stranger quite unknown to Grass and his party. In the novel, Grass has accepted an invitation to read and to participate in discussions at an Evangelical Church Congress in Stuttgart. At the meeting, Augst, having voiced a salute to his former comrades in the Nazi SS and denounced the church for rejecting his fellowship, ingests a bottleful of potassium cyanide. He dies, at age fifty-six, on the way to the hospital. Grass, profoundly affected by the incident, finds that he cannot dispose of Augst in a footnote, as he hoped to initially. Emotional impact, human sympathy, and inherent didacticism combine in moving Grass to pursue the history of Augst, which he reveals with agonizing slowness and effect, in bits and pieces juxtaposed for the next seventy pages with the story of Doubt and the account of the political campaign.

When Grass meets Mrs. Augst and the three Augst sons, eighteen, twenty, and twenty-two, he finds that each has her or his distorted but unembellished mental picture of the late husband and father. Now the listener rather than the storyteller, Grass is impressed by the honesty reflected in those divergent and often contradictory memories. Augst emerges as a sad paradigm of the Nazi generation, more victim than victimizer, his humanity stunted, his yearning to humanly "belong" perverted into membership in Nazi organizations. The downfall of Nazism left Augst as an anachronism, and without a trade or profession. In his forties he completed a pharmacy degree. Whether he had or had not been obsessed by the personality-cult aspect of

Hitlerism, after the war he was driven by the idea of community, by his need to communicate, and by his hunger for participation in public discussions.

Both early and late, however, Augst's obsession to communicate was thwarted by his literal inability to communicate, a heritage owing perhaps as much to Nazi conditioning as to innate factors of personality. Grimly he took elocution lessons to aid his single-minded efforts to effect community, to belong. Of diversions he had none, if we except the fact that he often went mushroom-gathering; but even that was not unrelated to his work as a pharmacist.

The gathering in nature, whether of mushrooms or snails, alerts us to a partial identity between Manfred Augst and Hermann Ott, of whom the two tales run side by side for almost one quarter of the novel. While it would not be critically accurate to push this identity into very many details, what does strike us is the dominance of utopian belief in both collectors: Ott's ill-considered absolute belief that melancolia could (and should) be completely curable; Augst's unconditional belief in political utopianism. Augst's belief brought him under the auspices of violence in the form of Nazism. His post-Nazi attempts to communicate were marked by violent speech and gestures. But ultimately his only act of violence was that perpetrated on himself, by means of the potassium cyanide.

*From the Diary of a Snail* consists of twenty-nine chapters and an epilogue entitled "Stasis in Progress. Variations on Albrecht Dürer's engraving Melancolia I. " This is in fact the Nuremberg lecture delivered by Grass in conjunction with the 1971 quincentenary of Dürer's birth, the lecture of which the novel itself is an outgrowth. Dürer's copperplate engraving *Melencolia I,* done in 1514, depicts in the foreground a heavy-set young woman with wings, sitting morosely among a clutter of discarded instruments and tools. In her hand rests a drawing compass in no very useful attitude, as though it too has been tried and found wanting. The background horizon is bright with the splendor of a radiant star, but little of the light gets to the twilightlike foreground, being somewhat obstructed by a building in which critics find some indication of incompleteness. Near the star in the background is a bat, across the back of whose outspread wings is inscribed the perhaps unsurprising title of the engraving. *Melancolia I.* (If the work was conceived as one of a series. Dürer never continued the series.)

Grass speculatively translates the woman in Dürer's engraving, who likewise bears the name Melencolia, into a variety of modern settings: in a cannery, on a chicken ranch, or at a conveyor belt. For, he says, melancholy has become the privilege of the wage earner subject to production quotas. According to Grass, melancholy in this role coincides with the utopian principle of absolute busyness. But even more is melancholy—the attitude or character trait seems undifferentiated from the affliction of melancholia—the privilege of an idle and arrogant elite, the power structure, whom the reader may be inclined to identify also as the parents of the young middle-class radicals given to denouncing Grass in the 1960s.

These social assignments of the character Melencolia remain speculative. Dürer's figure, in Grass's interpretation of the engraving, actually represents a reactive melancholy, springing, in her (and Dürer's) own humanistic age, from knowledge and self-understanding. The clutter about her can be taken to reflect the self-doubt of science. But she, brooding, represents what Grass in the subtitle of his lecture, and elsewhere in the novel, calls "stasis in progress," or, dialectically (hermaphroditically, in Grass's terminology), progress from stasis. Melancholy is necessary to progress, and progress is necessarily melancholic—and, as the novel declares, snaillike.

Utopia, whether as prescribed by the Soviet state or as sold by American television commercials, presupposes the corrective of melancholy. Both systems, the Soviet *and* the American, have outlawed melancholy. From this state of affairs proceeds the first of the two chief themes of *From the*

*Diary of a Snail,* in consonance with Grass's overt didactic intention: the middle-class family and its institutions, above all, its schools, have failed to inculcate in their children any corrective to utopian ideas. Such a corrective, to be discerned in melancholy and in the snail, he commends to his own and other people's children. Slowness is progress, not riots—or later, terrorism (which Grass foresees with uncanny accuracy).

Second, from the Danzig and German experience of fascism, of extremism, of political utopia: one connot afford to acquiesce to Nazi or Nazi-like terror, in either its pure form in the thirties or its later manifestation, whether from the right or the left, in the sixties, by pretending its nonexistence. The seedbed of extremism has not dried up. Opposition must be effective, which it was not in the thirties. Ideas avail little in the absence of courage.

*From the Diary of a Snail* is a complex and successful integration of diary and fiction, of the diarist and the fictive narrator. In this respect it foretells the increasingly prominent role of Günter Grass as author, as distinguished from fictive narrator, in his succeeding works of fiction. It cannot be denied that the lack of a fixed narrational point of view, or rather the presence of a multiple narrational point of view, may present difficulties for an inattentive reader. On the other hand, for a perceptive reader it presents additional perspectives of irony. Into the bargain, it may make didacticism, which Grass hardly lacks, significantly more acceptable.

It should probably be reiterated that this didacticism, which in his succeeding fiction will indeed become increasingly international in its scope, is nonetheless rooted in Grass's experience as a German author and as a German political thinker-practitioner of socialist persuasion and Social Democratic adherence. There is an irony as devastating as any that Grass himself delivers, in uncritically aligning him, even by implication, into the role of surrogate apostle of the American middle class and middle-class consumerism.

# 8

## Poetry

Even while he was studying at the Düsseldorf Academy of Art, Grass was writing poetry. And even as a world-renowned novelist he has continued to write verse, although more recently at a somewhat slackened pace. The German editions of his poetry almost always include drawings—by none other than that versatile artist, Günter Grass (who also does the cover designs for his poetry, as well as the no less relevant jacket designs for his prose works). The illustrations for his earliest poems are spare and angular, comprising a visual restatement of the poem—and are apt to be equally original. They do not symbolize, any more than do the poems themselves. Like the drawings, the poems dwell exclusively on objects—perhaps even human objects, but certainly not on the human soul, the preoccupation of many a German lyricist before Grass. Grass himself notes that the French *nouveau roman* contributed to his preoccupation with objects, as well as the spareness of early German expressionist verse.

Having attracted some attention for his poetry during a reading before Group 47 in 1955, Grass published his first volume, *Die Vorzüge der Windhühner (The Merits of Windfowl,* or sometimes *The Advantages of Moorhens),* in 1956, three years before the publication of *The Tin Drum.*

(Only certain selections from Grass's collections of poetry have been translated into English; I have accordingly retained the German titles of the collections while also giving the English titles as used by critics.) The volume of poetry had sold some seven hundred copies when the novel thrust Grass into worldwide prominence. Birds are indeed the subject of some of these early poems, but by no means all of them. In the early poems Grass's frequent technique is to isolate objects (including human and animal objects) and then to put them into unexpected associations with other objects. Thus, in "Open Air Concert":

> When the interval seemed to have been overcome
> Aurelia arrived with the bone.
> Look at my flute and my white shift,
> look at the giraffe peering over the fence,
> those are my blood, which is listening.
> Now I'll defeat all the thrushes.
>
> When the yellow dog ran over the meadow
> the concert expired.
> Later the bone could not be found.
> The scores lay under the chairs,
> the conductor seized his air-gun
> and shot all the blackbirds.

The poem seems to defy interpretation. (Grass, in fact, has a very low opinion of interpretation and intellectualization of art, whether graphic, plastic, lyric, or prose, deploring especially the tendency to regard literature as "a cow to be milked.") In "Open Air Concert" there seems to be a preoccupation with gold (Aurelia, the yellow dog; are they the same?) bones, or bone (anticipation of the Holocaust bone-pile in the novel *Dog Years*). There is indeed a juxtaposition, perhaps a blending under musical auspices of object, of animal, and of human. The fifth line contains a mild parody of biblical language, a technique also used in the novels. Finally, there are blackbirds *(Amseln)*, anticipating Eddi Amsel, a persona of one of the fictive joint authors of *Dog Years*. In general there is no consistent interpretation and in its stead, not untypically of Grass's early poetry, several inchoate motifs that reappear in later works much more fully adumbrated.

Grass called his second collection of poems, published in 1960, *Gleisdreieck (Railroad-Track Triangle)*, after that junction in Berlin before the erection of the Wall, when one could ride with relative freedom from East Berlin to West Berlin, and from West to East. Despite his acclaim as the author of *The Tin Drum*, Grass the lyricist of 1960 has hardly changed. He is still concerned with objects—above all, objects in unfamiliar surroundings. He is perhaps a trifle less playful than in his earliest poems—where however the playfulness seemed usually to have its grim obverse, sometimes patent, sometimes implied. And the accompanying drawings have now taken on size and the figures, predominantly animal or animallike, have taken on bulk and greater substantiality. The untranslated title poem "Gleisdreieck" unites the motifs of cleaning women riding on the train from the East Sector to the West Sector with that of a huge (to judge from the accompanying drawing) spider that lays and oversees the tracks.

"In the Egg" reiterates Grass's typically vague demarcation between man and animal (the unhatched chicks are highly articulate and evidently graphic as well). The poem also reflects his preoccupation with food and cooking—Grass is an excellent cook. The first, second, seventh, and eighth stanzas of the eight-stanza poem follow:

> We live in the egg.
> We have covered the inside wall
> of the shell with dirty drawings
> and the Christian names of our enemies.
> We are being hatched.
>
> Whoever is hatching us
> is hatching our pencils as well.

Set free from the egg one day
at once we shall draw a picture
of whoever is hatching us.


And what if we're not being hatched?
If this shell will never break?
If our horizon is only that
of our scribbles, and always will be?
We hope that we're being hatched.

Even if we only talk of hatching
there remains the fear that someone
outside our shell will feel hungry
and crack us into the frying pan with a pinch of salt.
What shall we do then, my brethren inside the egg?

We seem to be in, or near, the familiar precincts of the chicken-egg priority: which came first? As presented by Grass, the problem contains the implication that, either way, the cycle of existence doesn't have much sense or purpose. Even more noticeable—to be sure, exaggeratedly so when the central stanzas are not present—is the related change from the initial assumption of fixed, reliable order to the terminal assumption of doubt. The terminal doubt seems to be reinforced by the (externally) ironic possibility of being consigned to a frying pan even before the hatching that might or might not take place.

A poem from *Railroad-Track Triangle* that later finds its way into *The Tin Drum* is "The Sea Battle":

An American aircraft carrier
and a Gothic cathedral
simultaneously sank each other
in the middle of the Pacific.
To the last
the young curate played on the organ.
Now aeroplanes and angels hang in the air
and have nowhere to land.

Somewhat shocking—and probably not without a concomitant instillation in the reader of a sense of vicarious
daring—is the implied visual similarity between the two
massive and soaring structures of war and peace that
mutually destroy each other. That fanciful picture may well
lead to a more shocking, musically accompanied, conceptual
equation between the tower of war and the presumed tower
of peace (Grass is very far from being a friend of the
Catholic church). Finally, in what could be seen as a
reiteration of Grass's more familiar animal-man or object-
man identity, there is the identity of airplanes and angels
running out of fuel and having no place to land. Are war and
peace essentially indistinguishable?

The increasingly political Grass and his disenchantment
with what he regards as the ineffective if not downright
counterproductive protest movements of the late 1960s are
reflected in the 1967 collection, *Ausgefragt (Questioned)*. In
this collection is a group of highly political poems under the
general heading, "Zorn Ärger Wut" ("Wrath Anger Fury"),
of which "Do Something" is a good example. The first few
lines of the four-page poem follow:

> We can't just look on.
> Even if we can't stop anything
> we must say what we think.
> (Do something, Do something.
> Anything. Do something, then.)
> Indignation, annoyance, rage looked for their adjectives.
> Indignation called itself righteous.
> Soon people spoke of everyday annoyance.
> Rage fell into impotence: impotent rage.
> I speak of the protest poem
> and against the protest poem.

The theme and even the phraseology of "Do Something"
recur in the subsequent *Max: A Play* and in *Local
Anaesthetic*, the novel that further elaborates the play.

Also in the collection *Questioned* is the somewhat

uncharacteristic "Vermont," which, however, may be of especial interest owing to its locale:

> For instance green. A green at odds with green.
> Green creeps uphill and wins itself a market;
> here houses painted white go for a song.
>
> Whoever thought this up discovers
> new green for instance in perpetual
> instalments, never repeats himself.
>
> Tools lie around, all greenly overcome
> though rust had been their reddest resolution,
> iron when formed, now to be bought as scrap.
>
> We burned our way through woods, but the new green
> grew far too fast, much faster than
> and greener than for instance red.
>
> When this same green is broken up.
> For instance autumn: the woods put on
> their head adornenments and migrate.
>
> Once I was in Vermont, there it is green . . .

In its extended focus on the details of landscape "Vermont" is uncharacteristic of Grass. As a rule, if he concerns himself with landscape at all, it is only fleetingly. On the other hand, "Vermont" demonstrates his typical bent for objectivizing, in this case the colors green, white, and red (although green itself is an unfamiliar color in Grass's spectrum).

The appearance in 1971 of *Gesammelte Gedichte (Collected Poems)*, a compendium of poems from Grass's first three collections, suggests two things about his career as a poet. First, his fame as a novelist was bringing his poems to the attention of a much wider circle of readers. Second, that very fame as a novelist, taken together with the demands of being an active political campaigner, were evidently reducing his poetic output. Grass himself would dispute that assertion.

In 1974 he noted that he had been writing poetry for the last two years; further, that after completing a long prose work he always went back to poetry as a way of getting acquainted with and testing himself anew (not to forget, back to drawing as well). In any case, beginning in 1972 he was already busy with preliminary work on the monumental novel *The Flounder,* which was completed in 1977.

Grass's most recent poetic works are *Mariazuehren* (1973) *(Inmarypraise)* and *Liebe geprüft (1974) (Tested by Love).* The former, which was originally trilingual (German, English, and French), is available in a bilingual, English and German, edition. It is primarily an art book consisting of attractive and sometimes provocative montages of biographical photographs, drawings, and handwriting, introduced by an integrating, montagelike title poem. *Liebe geprüft* is a slim collection of etchings and accompanying verse.

# 9

## *The Flounder*

*The Flounder* is frequently said to mark Grass's return to literature. The implication is that he had been absent while pursuing politics. Probably a further implication is that his preceding work, *From the Diary of a Snail,* is more political than literary. As has been noted in chapter 7 above, that further implication is dubious. Even more unwarranted is the basic notion that if Grass were pursuing politics then he must not have been pursuing literature. In fact he began the preliminary work on *The Flounder* in 1972. By 1974 he was deeply involved in writing this great novel—the adjective applies to both its extent and its stature.

It may be surprising that he originally intended to subtitle his lengthy and complex work "Fairy Tale." In an interview coincident with the publication of the novel,[1] Grass asserts with delightful and perhaps predictable malice that he forbore such a subtitle so as not to handicap the dissemination and marketing of the novel. At the same time he flings a slightly disguised verbal dart at the role of academic criticism, implying its incomprehension of such an anomaly as a seven-hundred-page novel labeled a fairy tale.

A fairy tale is short and simple, and its hero may be immune to death. *The Flounder* is neither short nor simple, and even the identity of the "hero," not to speak of his

111

mortality, could be variously interpreted. The fairy tale on which *The Flounder* is based and which contains its central motif apparently came to Grass's attention in the early seventies. The tale is contained in the well-known collection gathered and written down by the Grimm brothers, Jacob and Wilhelm, in the early nineteenth century.

The Grimms' tale is about a fisherman and his wife, who live in a pisspot close by the sea. One day the fisherman catches a flounder. When the flounder declares that he is really an enchanted prince and would not make a delicious meal, the fisherman throws him back. In response to his wife's testy questions about the day's catch, the fisherman tells why he released the flounder. Go back, says his wife, and call the fish, for under the circumstances you are entitled to make a wish. The fisherman sees no need to make a wish. His wife seizes on this statement of contentment to announce that she, for one, is tired of living in a pisspot. She directs her husband to call the flounder back and convey her wish for a nice little cottage to live in. The fisherman complies. The flounder promptly grants his wish.

The wife does not long remain content in the new cottage. Yearning for a castle, she orders her husband to call the flounder again and relay her new wish. The wish is granted. Next she would become king, then emperor, then pope. At each stage her husband reluctantly relays her wish, and the flounder promptly grants it. Finally the wife, still discontented, aspires to become "like God," to be able to make the sun and the moon rise. When the amiable flounder hears that wish, he as usual tells the fisherman to go back home. But there he finds his wife living in the old pisspot. And there they are still living.

There is another version of this tale, however, and that lost version, according to Grass, is the basis of the novel—not the "misogynistic propaganda" contained in the tale above. About two-thirds of the way through the novel Grass gives background and details of the lost, alternative version of the fundamental tale. In this version the man rather than the woman is the discontented one, always wanting more and more, striving higher and higher. Despite the sensible advice of his wife Ilsebill, this insatiable fellow wants to rule the world with technology, to dominate nature, to travel to the stars. At the end of the tale, however, all his technological inventions, his impositions on nature, collapse and crumble as apocalyptic storms usher in a new ice age.

Which of the two versions of the tale is correct? the old woman who is the folk-informant is asked. "The one and the other," she replies. (Actually it reads, "The one and the other together" in the Low German original. The togetherness, indeed the interwovenness present in the narration by the old woman seems inadequately reflected in the Manheim translation.) To put it in terms of Grass's novelistic adaptation of the theme, female striving eventually leads to disaster equally with male striving—and this is particularly true when female striving is indistinguishable from that of males. Something new and different, a third way, is preferable, in fact essential, if the human race is to survive. The chance of such salvation, while doubtless remote on the basis of history to date, is not entirely precluded. There is still an open end.

The basic organizational unit in *The Flounder* is not chapter, book, or section—but month. There are nine of them in the book. The equivalence with the term of pregnancy for humans is fundamental rather than merely clever. The book is dedicated to Grass's daughter Helena, and if one takes the first-person narrator as a persona of himself, then the book runs from Helena's conception to her birth (encompassing as well the contemporaneous disintegration of Grass's marriage to Anna Grass). The novel also has potential endings, coinciding with possible live birth, in the seventh and eighth months. These potential endings—respectively with man resigned after his errors, or with woman replicating the errors of man—are then followed by the open ending of the birth. It is not necessarily a happy ending—the disquieting signs cannot be overlooked—but an ending with dialectical possibilities: there may be a third way. Each month of the novel, except the eighth, contains a number of title subdivisions (as many as twenty-two in the first). The subdivisions are frequently verse rather than prose.

The first month, in the course of which Grass describes the complex structure of the novel, begins with a sexual proposition, a human conception. Thus the novel promptly proclaims its chief theme: the relationship of men and women in an age, the mid-1970s, when the old assumptions about roles are no longer valid, but new roles are uncertain. In a word, the theme is role conflict between men and women. The second principal theme is food—the availability of food and the types of, preparation of, and consumption of food. The third theme is that of the basic fairy tales of the flounder: man's—or woman's—insatiable thirst for material advancement, with disaster the likely result unless change is effected. And by change Grass means fundamental change, not merely role-switching. The themes are interwoven with and counterbalance one another.

A subordinate theme playing through the chief themes is the relationship between reality and fiction. In Grass's view conventional history, based as it is on the written documents of special interests (for example, ecclesiastical), is in fact fiction. As a fiction writer, not relying on documentation reflecting special interest, Grass is able to invent facts of superior authenticity.[2] *The Flounder,* even more than *From the Diary of a Snail,* illuminates history with fiction— reverting here to conventional understanding of these terms—and fiction with history.

As the two conventional categories of narration, history and fiction, are in effect dissolved in *The Flounder,* so are the categories of conventional linear time. The past can occur together with, alongside, and flowing into the present; the present is no more actual than the past. In short the temporal mode is simultaneity. In the novel, events that happen centuries apart occur simultaneously. The dissolution of space is comparable, although on the whole less cosmic in effect.

The three primary seats of action are: first, the area around Hamburg, the evident abode of the first-person narrator and his wife Ilsebill; second, Danzig, the area around Danzig and the mouth of the Vistula, the familiar geography of most of Grass's previous writings; and third, Berlin. On a time scale running from the mythological Stone Age to sometime after the occasion in 1970 when the armed forces of Communist Poland killed Polish workers, Grass arrays three narrative levels. Each level has its own nucleus of characters, who, however interact not only on their own level but also with the characters of the other narrative levels. The first narrative level consists of the fictive first-person narrator and his wife Ilsebill. The second consists of a number of women cooks, historical and fictional, from various stages of Danzig prehistory and history, together with the men for whom they cooked and with whom they associated. The third level consists of a group of contemporary feminists, all fictional (though not without real-life prototypes), all female, sitting as a court in judgment of the captive Flounder, who is charged with having counseled men to those ideas of progress and dominance leading to the present ethical bankruptcy of western civilization and to the brink of human catastrophe.

As the novel progresses through the nine months of subdivisions, the nameless narrator, although preserving a single narrative consciousness, slips into the roles of the men most closely associated with the women cooks. In each of these incarnations the narrator also has at least one male friend or confidant. As for Ilsebill, she is to be found in many of the historical and fictional women cooks. Finally, each of the eleven women cooks through the ages (three in the first month, one in each succeeding month) is to be re-recognized in one of the eleven members of the Women's Tribunal (or the Womenal, as the Flounder calls it at the end of the novel).

In the first month, after the impregnation of Ilsebill by the narrator, the narrator slips into the character of one Edek, a late Stone-Age hunter and fisher. In the latter capacity on

May 3, 2211 B.C., a Friday, he catches the redoubtable
Flounder in an eel trap in Danzig Bay. Until that day Edek
has been contentedly under the matriarchal sway of a
Pomorshian mother of mankind, the three-breasted Awa.
(By "Pomorshian" Grass means the ancestors of the
Kashubians. The Slavic roots of the word simply mean "by
the sea," that is, the Baltic; the Latinized English equivalent
is Pomeranian.) In return for not having his self-acknowledged
tastiness brought to its succulent conclusion in a meal
prepared by Awa, the genial Flounder proposes to guide
Edek in throwing off the shackles of the matriarchy that has
prevailed for millennia. By taking advantage of the
Flounder's counsel, the male, dedicated to material progress,
will become the master of history. For example, a fire can be
used not merely for warmth and cooking, but for smelting.
Edek accepts the proposal. First, the male is to be weaned
from the paralyzing comfort of Awa's breasts; then to
undertake material progress, to hand down property, to
make war.

In the present time, the Flounder is caught again. His
captors are three women who, as Grass puts it, regard
themselves as lesbians and are therefore members of a
women's liberation group. They set up the Women's Tribunal
in an old movie theater to try the Flounder for the damage he
has wreaked on feminism over the millennia—that is, for
doing what he has promised Edek he would do. Flown to
Berlin on British Airways in his prison-tub the eloquent
Flounder points out that he is not so much for one
dominating gender-principle or the other as he is for change
per se. And now indeed, because change is desirable, he is
prepared to change his allegiance and to champion the
feminist cause. The Flounder at this stage is so ironic, so
clever, so grandly genial in his protestations that the
feminists are not inclined to accord them much belief.

It takes a very long time for Awa's matriarchy to lose its
grip on the male clientele of the Flounder in the region of the
Baltic Sea. In the Iron Age, the third century after Christ,

the Mediterranean regions, liberated from matriarchy, are far in advance of the Baltic in the fruits of the male principle: progress, property, and war. The peevish Iron-Age cook in the Baltic region is Wigga, and even there change is under way: Wigga has only two breasts.

The third and last cook in the first month is Mestwina. In the year 997 she drunkenly slays the evangelizing Bishop Adalbert with a cast-iron ladle. Adalbert's immediate mistake is in trying to take sexual advantage of Mestwina. His perhaps larger error consists in forcibly converting the Pomorshians to Christianity. In any case, it was with Mestwina—the Flounder assures the Women's Tribunal— that Awa's matriarchy finally came to its end. The counter-parts of Awa, Wigga, and Mestwina on the Women's Tribunal are: the presiding officer, Dr. Ursula Schönherr; the peevish Helga Paasch; and the constantly drunken Ruth Simoneit.

The first month, containing as it does Grass's preliminary sketch of the novel as a whole in addition to the narration concerned with the cooks and their associates and contempo-rary counterparts, comprises about one-fifth of the total novel. Each of the remaining eight months, proceeding from the basis of a single cook, is approximately half of the length of the first. In the second month the Tribunal discusses the Flounder's complicity in the case of the cook Dorothea von Montau (1346-94), also a religious fanatic, flagellant, and wife of swordmaker Albrecht Slichting, whose role is inhabited by the first-person narrator. The marriage becomes a hell for Slichting. Dorothea von Montau, celebrated cook, frigid wife, and uncaring mother of nine children, ignores husband as well as children in favor of her frequent bouts of religious ecstasy. She penultimately has herself walled up in the Marienwerder Cathedral (canonization cannot be afforded the living), where she survives for more than a year.

Dorothea von Montau's present-day alter ego on the Women's Tribunal is Dr. Sieglinde (Siggie) Huntscha, the determined prosecutor of the Flounder. Like Siggie, captor of the Flounder in the first month, Dorothea is closely involved with the intelligent fish, who in fact jumps into her arms from shallow water when she calls him. Dorothea distorts her mouth permanently by kissing the Flounder's slightly crooked mouth, although previously she has insisted that she would really be kissing her sweet Jesus merely in the form of a flounder.

In the second month the narrator as Günter Grass incorporates autobiographical detail into his fiction, as he does frequently throughout the novel. In this case it is detail based on and evoked by his filmmaking visit to the rebuilt Danzig in 1974. Among other reflections provoked by his visit: what kind of dialecticism is it by which on December 18, 1970, armed forces of the People's Republic of Poland fire on and kill Polish workers who have just been singing the "Internationale" or, as we are told in a fictionalized account in the ninth month, quoting aloud from the *Communist Manifesto*?

The cook in the third month is the abbess Margarete Rusch (1498-1585), whose counterpart on the Tribunal is Ulla Witzlaff, a Berlin organist. At the Rusch stage of the Flounder's trial several attempts are made to assassinate the defendant, who thereafter is afforded the protection of bullet-proof glass and communicates with his accusers by way of an intercom system. The latter proves by no means disadvantageous to his rhetorical style of speech, sprinkled now with Low German expletives.

Rusch, called Fat Gret, incorporates Oriental spices and pepper into her Danzig cuisine. The spice connection provides an opportunity for the narrator, as both Vasco da Gama and Günter Grass, to incorporate into the novel the history of the Portuguese seafarer's voyage to India as well as the history of the Danzig novelist's flying trip to India. Fat Gret, daughter of a blacksmith, is caught up in the political and religious machinations of the Protestant Reformation and the Catholic Counter-Reformation, in which machinations the guilds played an important role. But, as seems to be customary for the nonpatrician components of the social order, the guilds in the long run come out empty-handed.

During the turmoil Fat Gret manages to remain abbess of St. Bridget's and to hold her nuns together while members of the other Catholic religious institutions are deserting to Luther. Pastor Jakob Hegge, a "mangy goat" in Rusch's opinion, is the garrulous and pedantic leader of the Protestant forces, inciting the populace to personal violence on Catholics as well as the destruction of religious pictures, statues, carvings, and even altars. His adversary Rusch seems to be a worldly wise nun. She knows how to ingratiate herself with men, how to bend them to her will not only by her culinary but also by her erotic arts. Possibly pregnant by Hegge, she dresses him in her skirts when he is obliged to flee the turbulent city. When he can't make it over the city wall she impels his successful flight by biting off his left testicle. Scurrility is not in short supply in *The Flounder* and has drawn its share of critical objections. The point here is not scurrility, but rather how a resourceful and talented—and doubtless motivated—woman succeeds in surviving in the contentious male-dominated society promoted by the counsel of the Flounder.

The fourth month of the Flounder's trial bears on his complicity in the case of the cook Agnes Kurbiella (1619-89). The unfortunate but unlamenting Kurbiella's counterpart among the women of the Tribunal is the Flounder's defense counsel, Bettina von Carnow, who, ineffective at best, is often reduced to confusion and tears, not least by the Flounder's tendency to conduct his own defense. Kurbiella, having been gang-raped at the age of thirteen by Swedish cavalrymen during the Thirty Years' War, is thereafter not quite right in the head. But harmless and affectionate, she finds employment first in the kitchen of the cranky and burned-out painter, Anton Möller, an arrangement that soon is extended to the bedroom as well. Later Kurbiella divides her time between Möller and the half-invalid, artistically burned-out poet, Martin Opitz, to whom she likewise ministers in a dual capacity and with consummate considerateness. Both artists, historically a generation apart in age, are permeated by the "I" of the fictive narrator. Both artists die on Kurbiella, as do her children, all except Opitz's posthumous daughter Ursel, as daft as her mother, with whom she perishes in witch-burning flames in Moscow years later.

The Flounder is accused of encouraging both Möller and Opitz to enlist the services of Kurbiella, who as a cook is capable of ministering to tender stomachs and as a woman is capable of unconditional affection. In the Flounder's opinion Kurbiella as a Muse may also be capable of relighting the artistic fires of the burned-out artists to whom he has recommended her. The whole arrangement—especially Kurbiella's role as a potential Muse—is highly odious to the cool, rationalizing mind of the prosecutor, Dr. Sieglinde Huntscha. The Flounder finds himself pleading, with apologetic irony, for the cause of true love. Firing off a series of devastating questions at this inviting target, Huntscha demands to know if men likewise are eligible to serve as "professional Muses" in the fashion of Kurbiella. What is the wage scale? Are summits of artistic accomplishment beyond the reach of women on their own? To this last question the Flounder responds with a hesitant yes. To the accompaniment of heated denunciation he is found guilty of encouraging Möller and Opitz to derive artistic stimulation from their abuse of Kurbiella. There was even some remark made about pimping.

In the fifth month the Women's Tribunal considers the case of the Flounder vis-à-vis the serf and farm-cook Amanda Woyke (1793-1806). Woyke is responsible for popularizing the potato in Prussia for both culinary and therapeutic use, the latter of dubious merit. In this role and as the presiding genius of a farm kitchen that feeds en masse she is responsible for an agricultural—thence socioeconomic—revolution in Prussia. On one occasion she even plays hostess to the king, Frederick the Great, on an unheralded inspection of the prosperous state potato farm that Woyke serves. In addition to her talent at cooking potatoes, Woyke is a gifted storyteller. Her husband, inhabited by the first-person narrator, is August Romeike, veteran of Frederick's wars and now Inspector of Crown Lands for the king. August has made Amanda pregnant after each of the king's battles, so that she has been blessed with seven children.

The serf and farm-cook Amanda Woyke is a pen pal of the Massachusetts-born Benjamin Thompson, later Count Rumford, physicist, inventor of the Rumford stove, and later an administrator in Bavaria. The real Thompson studied at Harvard College and was a schoolmaster in Concord (formerly Rumford), New Hampshire. A royalist in the American Revolution, he fled Boston at the last moment. He played a part in the shameful sale of Hessian mercenaries to the British Crown before he moved on to Vienna and Munich. As a Bavarian administrator and a correspondent of Woyke he promotes potato cultivation in the rural areas of Bavaria as well as a workhouse geared to mass-feeding in Munich. Thus Woyke's vision of giant kitchens and a utopian potato soup dispensed the world over finds early application—possibly even preventing something like the French Revolution from happening in Bavaria.

The Flounder claims credit for bringing together in a pen-pal relationship the productive pair of Woyke and Rumford, who with their sponsorship of planned agriculture and mass-feeding could be regarded as proto-Maoists. Prosecutor Huntscha however bears down on the dubious argument *ex negativo,* that is, of preventing a revolution that didn't happen. She points out too that Rumford's Munich workhouse a few years later became a notorious jail. In short, demands the prosecutor, is the Tribunal to endorse a morality of specious boasting?

Proceeding from the carefully nurtured sub-theme of

Maoism, that is, a utopian cultural mass movement, the
narrator as himself introduces a telling parable to cap the
generally political tone of the fifth month (including Grass's
reminiscence of his presentation of "Seven Theses on
Democratic Socialism" at a convention in Bièvres, near
Paris, in February 1974). In the parable, the narrator is
taking a walk with Ilsebill, now five months pregnant.
Despite his anguished cry "don't jump," she attempts to leap
a five-foot ditch, barely makes it, but falls on the soft
ground, turning her belly to one side as she goes down. She
suffers no more than a turned ankle. Mao and China she
asserts, did not fear a Great Leap forward. You don't
progress much by crawling: "You with your snail philosophy."
The snail, of course, is Grass's model of progress.

In the sixth month the Women's Tribunal deliberates the
case of Sophie Rotzoll (1784-1849). The granddaughter of
Amanda Woyke, Rotzoll is the cook for Jean Rapp, Napo-
leon's military governor of Danzig, a witty, by no means
inhumane Alsatian. Some of the war-weary populace
maintain she is "Rapp's whore" as well. She is not, however.
Rotzoll remains a virgin her entire life. This is perhaps made
easier by the fact that the one love of her life, Fritz
Bartholdy, was imprisoned for thirty-eight years. Fritz's
status as a political prisoner endures from one political
regime to another despite the continued and insistent efforts
of Rotzoll to intervene in his behalf. They were teenage
sweethearts when Bartholdy was first incarcerated in 1797
for the expression of revolutionary sentiments inspired by the
then young French Revolution. Those sentiments were fully
shared by Rotzoll, who learns, however, as the Revolution
develops into Napoleonic imperialism, to modify her
repertoire of appropriate political songs (she is a talented
singer as well as a talented cook).

Rotzoll's tour de force as a cook occurs on September 26,
1813, as a revenge against those responsible, past and
present, for the imprisonment of Bartholdy and against
those who eat well while Danzigers go hungry. Her French

Revolutionary sympathies long attenuated, she is now a thorough German patriot. The French general, Rapp, who has refused her petitions for the release of Bartholdy, habitually has dinner guests from among the officers of the international forces occupying Danzig. For them Rotzoll prepares, among other delectable dishes, her specialty, a boned stuffed calf's head. The mushrooms for the stuffing—in this case mushrooms that destroy the human nervous system—have been smuggled to her by her cousin. All the diners but Rapp, who holds back from the pièce de résistance, are affected by a twitching of the facial muscles, then by a quarrelsome agitation. Violence erupts, sabers and carving knife go into action. Six guests die. Rapp, heartbroken at the necessary departure of Rotzoll, with whom he was never able to get anywhere amorously, arranges for her to go underground. The days of the French occupation draw to a close.

Before her tenure in the kitchen of General Rapp, and again after the collapse of the French power, Rotzoll is the cook for Pastor Blech, who has also interceded in vain for the release of Bartholdy. The first-person narrator inhabits all three of the male principals: Bartholdy, Rapp, and Blech. And as himself in the present time he shops with his pregnant wife Ilsebill for maternity wear at an Indian dress shop in Hamburg: an opportunity for some ironic and guilty reflections by two socially aware people on why the prices of Indian-made apparel are so reasonable. He introduces to his wife and home the members of the Women's Tribunal (with whom Ilsebill makes common cause against her husband) in a mushroom-induced hallucinatory reunion over a stuffed calf's head. Without benefit of mushrooms he invites to his home Associate Judge Griselde Dubertin, a pharmacist by profession, with an expertise in poisons, including those of mushrooms. Naturally Dubertin is the twentieth-century identity of Sophie Rotzoll. It might be said that Dubertin's poisoning role, figuratively speaking, is of Ilsebill against her husband—not that Ilsebill isn't already amply disgusted with him.

It is in this, the sixth month, that Grass introduces in considerable detail the narrative events surrounding variations of the fairy tale of the fisherman and his wife, one of the principal thematic bases of the novel. Correspondingly the reader sees somewhat less of the Flounder himself during this month. We do, however, find him offering the fundamental observation that whereas women bear children and thus live in their offspring, men, being unable to conceive, are forced "to do clever little tricks," such as build pyramids, dig Panama Canals, break sound barriers, and invent the pill. For this observation, supplemented by the prediction that women, with increasing equality, would become increasingly predisposed to masculine baldness, the Flounder is roundly condemned by the Tribunal as a reactionary.

By the seventh month the Flounder's historical support of the male cause is flagging, his role as adviser more and more neglected. The prosecutor, Dr. Huntscha, reproaches him for failing to prevent either of the husbands of the people's cook Lena Stubbe (1848-1942) from beating her when they get drunk on payday. The husbands, both of them inhabited by the narrating "I," are, successively, Friederich Otto Stobbe, killed in the Franco-Prussian War, and Otto Friederich Stubbe, killed in World War I—the not untypical fates of socialist workers who rushed to arms in behalf of German imperialistic expansion. The member of the Women's Tribunal paired with Lena Stubbe is Erika Nötke, a social worker, a self-educated, class-conscious socialist and Social Democrat.

Grass's political preoccupation reemerges emphatic_lly during this month. Surviving her beatings at the hands of her thereafter whimpering husbands, and cooking, cooking, cooking—not to mention reading and reading and writing and writing—Lena Stubbe idolizes the chairman of the Social Democratic party, the historical figure August Bebel. The two biggest events of her life are bound up with Bebel, who is familiar with her reputation as a party bulwark and a famous cook. While on a political trip to Danzig, Bebel pays a visit to the Stubbes in their proletarian duplex. After her excellent dinner he stays to talk with Lena. She tries to persuade him to write a foreword for her long-nurtured project, "The Proletarian Cookbook," whose purpose is to persuade working-class women not to imitate middle-class cooking but to validate their proletarianism in their cooking. Without the endorsement of Bebel she has no chance of successfully publishing the book. Unfortunately he feels obliged to refuse, for the good of the party; such an endorsement would expose him to bourgeois ridicule and so weaken the party. By now Bebel is glancing significantly at his pocket watch—the same watch, Grass informs us, that Willy Brandt now carries on festive occasions. Stubbe is hurt but not disillusioned.

In 1913 as a representative of the Danzig Social Democrats, Stubbe undertakes a train trip from Danzig through Germany to Zurich, there to attend Bebel's funeral. Grass implicitly identifies the death of Bebel in 1913 with the resignation of Bebel's ideological successor and Grass's friend, Willy Brandt, from the chancellorship in 1974 upon the disclosure that the Communists, who are said to spy on one another and everyone else as well, had a man—Günter Guillaume—in Brandt's inner circle. Grass implies that both events, the death of one leader and the resignation of the other, were tragedies for the Social Democratic Party. Many, many years later Lena Stubbe meets her death in the concentration camp at Stutthof, near Danzig, while still ladling soup at the age of ninety-four, evidently murdered by a common criminal, a favored class in the Nazis' concentration camps.

The eighth month, a departure from the overall construction of the novel, is the critically notorious "Father's Day." Here Grass melodramatically comes to grips with lesbianism as a false direction just as inhumane as the machoism that the Flounder has been promoting. Both the

effect and the narrative technique of the eighth month—
cuts, pans, camera angles, flashbacks, montages—are
essentially cinematic; lest the reader be inclined to overlook
that fact and perhaps lament the absence of the usual
narrative subdivisions and guideposts, Grass incorporates
ample internal reminders.

The cook is Dr. Sibylle Miehlau (1929-63), called Billy,
the great-granddaughter of Lena Stubbe. She is a lawyer by
profession but has always liked to cook. She is the
designated cook on the fatal Father's Day picnic in the
woods with the three friends who share her lesbian preference,
including Dr. Sieglinde Huntscha, the prosecutor for the
Women's Tribunal. (Miehlau was once the girlfriend of the
first-person narrator; they have a ten-year-old daughter).
The narrator has also enjoyed satisfactory (to him) sexual
relations with two of the other women, but they have had
enough of his and other male selfishness and have turned to
their own sex.

The female picnic on Father's Day is anomalous and
ironic in the context of a day consecrated in Berlin to
exclusively male outings. Men turn out in clubs, associations,
fraternities, and motorcycle gangs to escape their Ilsebills for
the day. The lakeshore and woods about the Miehlau picnic
site are infested with ten, no, a hundred thousand males. A
nearby fraternity, and also a motorcycle gang, are offended
by the presence of women. Especially is the gang offended,
but also aroused, by the sexual activity that they witness,
culminated by Billy Miehlau's three companions raping her
in turn as she sleeps. Except that she awakens and futilely
resists the third. Crying, disgusted, proclaiming herself a
woman, Miehlau flees on foot into the woods. Not very far.
Seven members of the motorcycle gang hunt her down and
encircle her with their bikes. After all seven have raped her
and kicked her around on the ground, they nudge her with
their throttled-down bikes. Finally, at full throttle, they run
over her legs and belly and kill her.

Melodramatic the eighth month is, and scurrilous as well

in details not recounted here. At first glance there is no artistic subtlety. Grass even uses the masculine pronoun to disparage the lesbian rapists of Sibylle Miehlau. That apparently blunt irony, however, is also double-edged or even triple-edged. On a narrative level it anticipates Miehlau's next set of attackers even as it reflects the hopelessness with which Grass regards the male cause. But the chief point on which Grass has been censured is of course the equation that he makes between lesbianism and the women's liberation movement.

The cook in the ninth month is Maria Kuczorra, born in 1949, cousin of the narrator and fiancée of Jan Ludkowski. She is a purchasing agent and cook at the Lenin Shipyards at Danzig, where Jan Ludkowski is a fellow employee. On December 18, 1970, while Jan, a trade-union and Communist League member is quoting from the *Communist Manifesto* in front of the shipyard gate—there was a strike owing to a sudden 30 to 50 percent increase in the price of staples—he is shot and killed by the police of the People's Republic of Poland. As in the case of Sibylle Miehlau, the Flounder also declines responsibility for the plight of Maria Kuczorra, the mother of twin daughters by Jan Ludkowski.

Conceivably as a result of his prolonged confinement in his prison-tub the Flounder is becoming more and more transparent as the Tribunal's verdict approaches. His final statement lacks any hint of the droll anecdotes with which he was formerly wont to make his points. He renounces his support of the male cause, which under the aspect of material progress has brought strife and suffering. Power, he predicts, will go to women; the turning point is now. He offers his counsel to women if the Womenal will have it. That body comes to a contentious split verdict. After a symbolic feast in which eleven flounders are ceremoniously consumed in full view of their distraught fellow, the Flounder is released at his preferred site in the Baltic, within view of the island on which the fairy tale of the Flounder originated.

Ilsebill bears a daughter. Her resentment at her husband's

absences to attend the trial, banquet, and release of the Flounder grows to fury when three months after the birth of their daughter the narrator, like Grass after the birth of his daughter, goes to Danzig, that is, Gdańsk, for the shooting of a television documentary on the reconstruction of the city—and to see (here it is the narrator again) Maria Kuczorra. At the end of the novel Kuczorra wades out into the sea up to her knees. As she shouts a Kashubian word three times, the Flounder jumps out of the water into her arms. He is *her* Flounder now. Although the narrator understands nothing of their conversation, it is clear that she is asking, and the Flounder is offering, counsel.

In accordance with Grass's principle of gradual, even snaillike change, the reader hopes that the Flounder's advice is not merely to emulate the male principle. The recent birth suggests synthesis, however difficult. On the other hand, when Maria's conversation with the Flounder is over, Maria—only it isn't Maria now—walks back, she— Dorothea von Montau, Agnes Kurbiella or Sophie Rotzoll or Billy Miehlau—overlooks the narrator, walks right past him. Is the Flounder ruining things again already? To be sure, change is required. But . . . .

The discussion of the events of *The Flounder* month by month has given only an approximate indication of the synchrony—also a kind of synthesis—that Grass evokes. With each succeeding month the characters and events of the preceding months do not disappear from view, but recur repeatedly in ever more detailed and closely woven relationships to each other. In this elaborate and skillful narrative dialecticism the controlling figure is the narrator, in the roles of the chief male figures as well as that of the regulator of the varied, sometimes extremely lengthy, autobiographical insertions.

These insertions, and other narrative embedding as well, come close sometimes to exhibitionism, as critics have not failed to observe. For example, the disintegration of Grass's first marriage, easily inferred from the novel virtually from beginning to end, has an uncomfortable, perhaps even painful effect on the reader. On the other hand it may be urged that the failing marriage is part of the essential interwoven material of the whole novel, which perhaps would not have existed otherwise—certainly not in its present degree of complexity and irony.

The motif of relationship, disintegrating as well as integrating, pervades *The Flounder*—it could hardly be otherwise in a novel whose theme is the desperate primary relationship between men and women, women and men. It has to do not only with marital relationship, but also with blood relationship, sexual relationship, identical relationship, affinitive relationship, epistolary relationship, political relationship, and combinations of all of these. But in the long run it comes down to the relationship between the sexes.

The Flounder identifies the recent turning point in the restoration of power to women. But Grass insists that an alternative mode is essential to the survival of the human race. If female striving is to become indistinguishable from male striving, then nothing whatever is gained. In making that valid point it may seem that Grass has proceeded less than evenhandedly vis-à-vis the two sexes. Not, certainly, that he is indulgent about the mess that men have made of things: it could hardly be more desperate. Still, Grass leaves himself open to the accusation of unfairness by allowing it to appear, if not contriving for it to appear, that there is an equation between feminism—or at least feminism as the bearer of the torch of power—and lesbianism. Men are brought into no such implicit, parallel equation. The macho motorcycle-gang members, murderous as they are, seem a rather light counterweight, far from sufficient to redress the imbalance.

That is probably a cavil when related to Grass's overriding theme that it is perilously late and some new mode is required in the distribution and exercise of power between the sexes. It is certainly a cavil when related to the sheer sweep of this intricate and yet monumental novel. *The*

*Flounder,* which demands even more of the reader, is a novel of the rank of *The Tin Drum.*

# 10

## *The Meeting at Telgte*

Only two years after the publication of the monumental
novel, *The Flounder,* Grass published *The Meeting at
Telgte* (1979, 1981). Much shorter, this story (Grass does
not call it a novel) is in fact a spin-off from *The Flounder.*
Grass developed and expanded the episode in the novel in
which the two baroque poets, Martin Opitz and Andreas
Gryphius, meet during the Thirty Years' War, specifically
on September 2, 1636. Martin Opitz (1597-1639), a translator
and poet, is most influential as a poetic lawgiver in his *Book
on German Poetry* (1624), in which he espouses neoclassic
rules of restraint and verisimilitude. Andreas Gryphius
(Gryf) (1616-1664), a writer of baroque religious poetry
especially evoking the horror of the Thirty Years' War, was
the greatest German dramatist of the seventeenth century.

For *The Meeting at Telgte,* the meeting of the two poets is
expanded to include practically every mobile poet in the
pantheon of German baroque literature, as well as two
musicians and several publishers. The date is advanced to
1647, one year before the end of the tenacious Thirty Years'
War, in which the German states, as the cockpit of European
religious, political, and military struggles, were subjected to
extreme destruction.

The significance of advancing the date to 1647 is twofold.

131

First, the war is almost over, there have been recent, aborted peace conferences, Germany is divided, prostrate, and powerless—thus in a situation analogous to what it was a bit after the end of World War II, that is, exactly three centuries later, in 1947. Second, the fictive meeting in Telgte (a small town on the Ems River between Münster and Osnabrück) is thereby clearly related to the actual meeting of the group of writers called Group 47 in 1947. The direction of relationship runs in both directions. On one level, the real meeting in 1947 is the model for the fictive meeting in 1647. But once we assume the fictional reality of the 1647 meeting, then chronologically the fiction becomes a model for the later reality, a model supported by a texture of allusive detail.

Grass dedicates *The Meeting at Telgte* to Hans Werner Richter on the latter's seventieth birthday, November 12, 1978. Richter is the father of Group 47, established in 1947 and dissolved, over the question of response to the student protests and increasing commercialization, in 1967. As Richter was the guiding genius and spirit of Group 47, so Grass makes the figure of Simon Dachital, a poet of the seventeenth century, the organizer and sponsor of the meeting at Telgte. The story contains allusions to the significance and cross-significance of the last names of the parallel figures: *Richter* in German means "judge," *Dach* means "roof, shelter, protection," so that each proper name can be brought into a relationship with the role of its bearer in the one meeting and with the analogue of its bearer in the other meeting.

Grass, it will be recalled, had a sympathetic relationship with Group 47 dating from the mid-and late 1950s, when the Group was receptive to his early verse and then put an early imprimatur on his *Tin Drum*. By the mid-fifties the Group was already a potent force in German literature. It arose originally, as Hans Werner Richter himself describes it, as a protest on the part of writers returned from war against what they regarded as the reactionary aestheticism then prevailing, whose roots went directly back to the nineteenth century and whose practitioners were apt to be compromised by having accommodated to Nazism in small or large degree. Moreover, the new writers—even if they wrote verse they did not want to be called poets—wanted nothing to do with a literary atmosphere characterized, in their view, by pious silence and candlelight. The new writers wanted to come to terms with a literature of the present in an honest and direct way, to read aloud to each other their works in progress, to expose themselves to collegial criticism.

Acting upon a consensus of disgust with anachronistic standards and of support for reform, Hans Werner Richter undertook to be the moving force in arranging a meeting of the new writers. Grass, a member from 1955, was never reticent about his reciprocal esteem for Group 47. *The Meeting at Telgte* is a fictional testimony to his esteem, which is deep enough to permit him a complete picture, warts and all—even if three centuries removed.

The general reader probably has some notion of the situation in Germany near the end of the Thirty Years' War. What had begun in 1618 as a war between adherents of Catholicism and Protestantism, with rulers of the several German states lining up on the one side or the other, had turned into a political war with the major European powers (including Sweden, excluding England) intervening militarily on German soil. Germany was physically, socially, and economically devastated. The German language itself was becoming creolized and was in danger of going under. At the same time, as sometimes happens under such circumstances, literary culture was represented by a quite remarkable and productive group of writers—in this case, generally baroque and mystic in tone.

While the study of German baroque literature has flourished recently, the panorama that Grass lays before us in *The Meeting at Telgte* is not exactly familiar to even the literate German reader. Part of this less than perfect familiarity is a result of the natural limits of even a very literate reader's expertise. But another factor is undoubtedly

Grass the autodidact's unusual immersion in and familiarity with the literature of the seventeenth century and with the men who wrote it. It has been said that in *The Meeting at Telgte* he displays a grasp superior to that typical of a German university seminar. In plainer terms, quite a number of perhaps not completely familiar names are borne by the group of writers who in Grass's work of fiction meet in Telgte in 1647.

At the instance of Simon Dach, the counterpart of Hans Werner Richter, they come from far and wide in Germany, and Grass dutifully catalogues their travels. One, Weckherlin, even came from London, where he had long been attached to the government. Two came from Jutland. Others, Moscherosch and Schneuber, for example, came from Strasbourg. Czepko, Logau, Hoffmannswaldau, together with a young man with an eye for the girls, then known as Johann Scheffler, came from Silesia. Johann Rist came from Wedel on the Elbe, by way of Hamburg. Paul Gerhardt, the Protestant hymnist, no friend of literature, came from Berlin. Dach himself came from Königsberg (now Kaliningrad in the Soviet Union) as did Gryphius, who however had been traveling in the west when he received Dach's invitation. Harsdörffer and Birken came from Nuremberg.[1] The latter pair were accompanied by, in addition to a publisher, one Christoffel Gelnhausen. Gelnhausen was later to emerge on the literary front as Hans Jacob Christoffel von Grimmelshausen (about 1622-1676), Günter Grass's admired master, author of the most famous German work of literature in the seventeenth century, the largely autobiographical *Adventures of Simplicius Simplizissimus* (1669), a picaresque novel after the original Spanish model.

The Nuremberg publisher was but one of several at the writers' meeting in Telgte in 1647. Their presence was both a reflection and a prediction of the later situation in Group 47. Publishers attended the sessions of Group 47 in increasing numbers, even intervening in the program-making in order to increase sales. The encroachment by the publishers was a major reason, along with the student protests (actual invasion of the meeting) for the disbanding of the Group in 1967.

It is Christoffel Gelnhausen, about twenty-five years old at this point, a military freebooter with political influence, a survivor by virtue of his wits and his chutzpah, and probably his amorality, who comes to the rescue of the assembled writers when the inn reserved by Dach proves to have been taken over by a Swedish military headquarters. Gelnhausen, at the head of a small contingent of Imperial (supposedly Catholic) troops, arranges for the writers to stay in an inn operated by his sometime mistress, Libuschka. Called Courage by Gelnhausen, she is a tough yet amiable woman, who later emerges as the adventuress Courage in Gelnhausen-Grimmelshausen's epochal and epoch-making novel, *The Adventures of Simplicius Simplizissimus*. And of course she was Mother Courage in Bertolt Brecht's drama of the same name. In the case of Courage's other name, Libuschka, it is useful to note that—although the name could also be purely Slavic—Grass gives the impression of effecting an East-West linguistic synthesis, adding—*uschka*, a Slavic suffix expressing tenderness or endearment, to a German word *Li(e)b*- that already means "love" or "dear."

The writers, some of them morally uncomfortable at Gelnhausen's dubious background and tactics, not to speak of his Imperial affiliations, settle in for their three-day meeting. The agenda, arranged by Dach, will have them discussing the state of literature and each other's literary readings, as well as the misery of their war-ravaged country, prolonged by aborted and dilatory peace negotiations. Not at all a monolithic group, they are diverse not only from a regional standpoint but also as individuals and writers. They subscribe to a variety of Catholic and Protestant credos and reflect various degrees of tolerance and intolerance. As they have religious and regional antipathies, so also are they subject to personal antipathies. They belong to a variety of

sometimes rival regional societies devoted to the cause of
German literature and to the preservation of the German
language. Their ages vary as does their devotion to sexual
activity with the maids of the establishment and with
prostitutes brought in from town. In other words, Dach's
entourage consists of diverse individuals brought together by
a common concern for letters (thus their language) and for
their country.

Many of their literary critiques are subsumed under an
intense desire to save the common language from becoming
creolized, as a series of foreign armies and their camp
followers crisscross the country. As for the German dialects,
to which some of the writers cling and which may contribute
to the vigor of a common language, they are too often
mutually unintelligible to serve as a substitute for the
common language. The various regional literary and language
societies with the picturesque names—for example, the
Upright Fir Tree Society—to which many of the writers
belong, have struggled to maintain the viability of the
common literary language. Even in their varying theories and
practice of literature, the assembled writers are highly
conscious of the plight of their medium. Self-interest is not
absent in this concern, but patriotic interest dominates.
Gelnhausen, the writer of the future, so to speak, destined to
be the most celebrated of them all, cannot comprehend the
all too frequent quarrels between the adherents of one
dialect and another. All of the dialects, in his opinion,
should continue to exist alongside one another as well as
mixed with one another.

Perhaps fulfilling our expectations, Grass the cook, Grass
the gourmand, does not, in *The Meeting at Telgte,* ignore
the pleasures of the board any more than he does those of the
book and the bed. His assembled writers dine both simply
and splendidly, and in neither case are we deprived of a
lovingly detailed menu. When the hostess Libuschka's larder
is depleted, Gelnhausen militarily appropriates or—as the
hungry writers are uncomfortably, but not too uncom-

fortably, aware—steals (and not only food). The last meal is comprised of a variety of fish caught by one of the writers who fished overnight in the Ems. At first it didn't appear that there was all that much, but . . . . The slightly blasphemous biblical analogy, a favorite device of Grass, is clear.

The writers drink in moderation, possibly because Libuschka possesses no great supply of beer. They find the dark beer at hand to their taste both for drinking and for after-dinner discussion, not excluding coarse jokes. This is true except for the youngest writers, who prefer to chase the three maids of the establishment, with whom they finally bed down in the straw of the attic. (Libuschka's inn does not have quite enough bedrooms for all the writers, even with doubling up.)

Beginning on the second day of reading and criticism, the writers read aloud from their works from the vantage point of a footstool, near which stands a potted thistle dug from the hostess's garden. The thistle is the consensual symbol of the war-torn era and country in which they live. By itself, isolated from other plants, the thistle is beautiful, and who can deny that it is durable? When at the final session, the poet and dramatist Andreas Gryphius in a fit of rage and frustration at the plight of Germany, seizes the pot with the thistle and shatters it on the floor, *that* is Germany. Amongst the shards the thistle itself remains whole, however, a significance not lost on the aroused assemblage.

There have been mumblings during the meeting about the desirability of the assembled writers making their weight felt on the political level, especially in getting effective negotiations under way among the many contending forces that have destroyed Germany. The trouble is that the writers have precious little weight in politics. What influence they might have is vitiated by the economic necessity of grinding out adulatory verse in exchange for the honorariums of the politically powerful. Still, some of the politically sensitive if powerless writers have composed initial drafts of a manifesto—a demand, in effect, that peace be proclaimed. Fights among the writers of the various demands for peace, the wise Simon Dach recognizes, are all too likely, and he admonishes his colleagues to calm. Perhaps predictably it is Logau, the epigrammatist, who denounces most vehemently the pomposity and the bourgeois triviality contained in the two semifinal drafts. But in general, calm is made to prevail.

Only the old Weckherlin—a veteran of years of political experience as an undersecretary of state in the English establishment—has any practical political knowledge, has experienced at first hand the play of political force and counterforce, has perhaps even personally affected those forces from time to time. As a uniquely aware writer-politician, Weckherlin to some extent resembles Günter Grass, above all in the insight that only very small, gradual increments of improvement are possible, that a grand solution is out of the question. Some air of resignation may inhere in such insight. It is certain that resignation is in the air as the meeting in Telgte draws to a close. That is not necessarily bad. Resignation, Grass noted some years before *The Meeting at Telgte,* is a useful, even a necessary thing. For without an attitude of resignation there can be no insight.

A new manifesto is composed on the spot by Simon Dach, and written down by Daniel Czepko. It is a restrained, sensible document that addresses the realities in its call for peace. It avoids name-calling, it affirms the patriotism of the assembled German writers as well as their concern that the possible political dismemberment of Germany will lead to its eventual end as a recognizable entity. It ends with a prayer for God's blessing, by writers both Protestant and Catholic. However, the signed manifesto, the one tangible common product of the meeting in Telgte, is destroyed in a devouring fire that breaks out at the inn after the final midday meal. The writers escape with their lives, but the inn is a total loss, along with the manifesto, which had been forgotten in the fish bones and the exuberance of the dining hall. It is not a matter of importance, the first-person narrator judges, for no one in power would have paid attention to it anyway.

The identity of the first-person narrator is both ambiguous and flexible. From prejudicial remarks about women at the meetings of the Nuremberg literature and language society it is assumed he is a male. He is generally inconspicuous, only rarely calling attention to himself, but evidently omnipresent and omniscient. Certainly he is omnipresent in 1647, for in response to his own rhetorical question of how he should know, for example, that a meal consisted of such-and-such courses, or that Libuschka sent her maids into town to recruit whores for the night, he replies simply that he was around. He appears to be present in 1978 as well, for he notes on one occasion that he has the benefit of hindsight as to Gelnhausen's subsequently (to 1647) becoming a celebrated writer of picaresque novels. In this remark we also detect in the first-person narrator the Günter Grass who so much esteems those novels of Gelnhausen-Grimmelshausen. Counterbalancing the identificational possibilities, the ambiguity of the narrator is reinforced by the pervasive stylistic device of indirect statement, marked in German by the consistent use of subjunctive verb forms. The use of indirect discourse permits the narrator, at his discretion, to distance himself from what is being narrated, as well as to comment informatively and sympathetically-ironically over his speakers' shoulders. In short, like Oskar in *The Tin Drum*, the "I"-narrator in *The Meeting at Telgte* is both "I" and Günter Grass.

In the very first line of *The Meeting at Telgte* Grass sets the tone of identity between past and present with the predictive, thought-provoking assertion that yesterday will be what tomorrow has been. On comparing that with the statement in *Local Anaesthetic* (and in *Max: A Play*) that what comes afterward is already contained in what comes before, the reader may note that the two formulations, paradoxical as it may seem at first, actually confirm and complement each other in the essential formulation of

continuity between past and present or, in the other
direction, between present and past. At the same time, each
statement is a highly concise summary of the work of which
it is a part. The fictive meeting at Telgte yesterday,
yesteryear, in 1647, is, or reflects, what has occurred in 1947,
1955, 1958, and 1967, that is, the formation of Group 47,
Grass's joining, Grass's reading from *The Tin Drum,* and
finally, dissolution.

One of the more striking aspects of identity between 1647
and, say, 1947, especially in the literary realm, is that of the
language in which writers write—the literary language, the
national language. The linguistic predicament in Germany
toward the end of the Thirty Years' War was anything but
encouraging. To make very sure the reader keeps that in
mind, Grass makes it a repeated thematic preoccupation of
his assembled writers. In no small measure due to the efforts
of Grass himself, the recovery of German as a literary
language during the past thirty-five years may blind us to the
fact that exactly three centuries after 1647, thus in 1947, the
language was also in dire straits. It had been so corrupted by
the propaganda language of Hitler's Germany, to a lesser
extent by the cautious, self-protective tone of even the less
suborned writers who elected to stay in that Germany, that it
had largely lost its ability to function as a mode of honest
communication. True, the technical details of the debauching
of language were not identical in the two eras. But it is more
importantly true that there was an identity between 1647 and
1947 in the sensing of the profound need to revive and
reinvent the national language.

Grass's dedication of *The Meeting at Telgte* to Hans
Werner Richter, the entire initial paragraph that amplifies
that dedication, the formulation of the identity between past
and present, present and past, may tempt us to regard and
interpret the work as a simple roman à clef, a novel, a story
in which actual persons are depicted in fictional guise. But
the only figure in the fiction who actually appears completely
or substantially modeled after a living person is the

organizer of the meeting in Telgte, the mediator between hotheads, the Silesian poet Simon Dach. The model is of course Grass's friend, Hans Werner Richter. The other baroque writers, who accept Simon Dach's invitation to the meeting, are pastiches, blends of what may be known of the historical writers whose names they bear, fictional invention, and even certain characteristics of living persons. As such they may be partially identifiable, thus not really identifiable, with living persons. Needless to add, however, there has been no dearth of resourceful critical attempts to effect identification.

But the identificational games hardly touch on the essential purport of *The Meeting at Telgte*. That is the clear recognition that writers are all but without influence in politics. And this is true even if they have a rehabilitated and vigorous language at their disposal. Is it mere accident that the only writer at the meeting in Telgte with genuine political knowledge and ability is the expatriate Georg Weckherlin, who is politically effective in a completely alien linguistic environment, that is, in England? The revised manuscript drawn up for ratification at the final session at the inn may have been superior to the early drafts, but that is inconsequential, because it was in any case left to be incinerated with the fish bones. And even had it been saved, so we are told, it would have made no real difference politically.

It is but one step from this recognition—or perhaps it is the same step—to identify Günter Grass's growing personal perception in 1978 and 1979 of the writer's inability to sway political developments very much. That is something like resignation, but with resignation comes insight. One may say that perception is especially valid when the writer, for example, Grass, profoundly mistrusts and disdains the ideologies that paralyze politics. On the other hand, while the writer cannot do very much, with luck and diligence he may be able to do a little. For example, most recently, speaking out against renewed American intervention in

Latin America may, in combination with many other factors, help confine its extent and scale.

In a reductive view, then, *The Meeting at Telgte* might appear as basically a political tract. But that would imply our having ignored the highly visible linguistic-literary dimension, together with the thoroughgoing personal irony at the expense of the assembled writers—irony that may in turn anticipate, but does not then yield the field to, the irony of the writer's plight as a player in the political contest.

## 11

## *Headbirths or The Germans Are Dying Out*

In *Headbirths* (1980) Grass continues to develop the narrative
mode common to *From the Diary of a Snail, The Flounder,*
and *The Meeting at Telgte:* the narrator mixes into the
material that he is narrating. Related to that intervention is
simultaneity. And spatial multiplicity, or simultaneity,
achieves a worldwide scale in *Headbirths.* Grass gives us not
only frequent direct reporting and reflecting on his own trip
to China and way points, but also has his fictional pro-
tagonists, Harm and Dörte Peters, participate in a tour to
India, Thailand, and Indonesia. Harm and his wife Dörte,
high-school teachers from Itzehoe, are able to take such an
extended tour, Grass informs us, because their summer
vacation is long enough to permit it, because midsummer is a
period between elections (in which they are both active
campaigners), and because they cannot come to a decision
about whether to have a child.

The parallel autobiographical trip to China via Cairo,
Singapore, and Manila is likewise undertaken, as characters
in the novel, by Grass and his second wife, the former Ute
Grunert. The Grasses are in the frequent company of Volker
and Margarethe Schlöndorff, who likewise appear as
characters in the novel. The movie director, Schlöndorff, and
Grass, who worked together on the filming of *The Tin
Drum,* intend to shoot some footage in China if they can

secure the necessary governmental permission. Since his close association with Schlöndorff we note that Grass has displayed a quickened interest in the artistic interrelationship of prose and film, revealed most notably in the filmic adaptation of the first two-thirds of *The Tin Drum* and in the "Father's Day" chapter in *The Flounder.* Now, in the first few pages of *Headbirths,* Grass speculates that the work could be a film, or a book, or both. Throughout the work of fiction he adduces the additional fiction that it is a film, by using such phraseology as "crosscuts," "in another scene," or even more plainly, "the film."

What does he mean by the curious title *Headbirths?* In general he means an idea, a fiction, a speculation. For readers who have the opportunity to see Grass's jacket sketch, that idea is represented on the front cover by a curled-up fetus, somewhat resembling the configuration of the human brain, lodged in, or on, the appropriate place on a human head. The fetus appears to be eating a sausagelike string of fecal material, or perhaps an umbilical cord. Seen as another portion of a human brain, that material might also be construed as a convolution—or perhaps we are not obliged to seek such precise identification. In any case the effect remains highly ironic. On the back cover the fetus is replaced by a huge egg. For readers who have perhaps an unsure grasp of classical mythology, Grass good-naturedly notes that his title refers to the way that the goddess Athena was born from the head of Zeus, "a paradox that has impregnated male minds to this day." That is to say, male minds have ever speculated, tossed off ideas.

Grass presents his thematic headbirth in the first paragraph. In Shanghai, a city of eleven million inhabitants, it occurs to him and Ute to speculate about what the world would be like if the population figures for Germany (both West and East Germany) and China were reversed. That fanciful world would then contain 950,000,000 Germans and a bare 80,000,000 Chinese. In the first place, he ironically reflects, it would take a revival of Prussian administrative genius to govern almost a billion Germans. But that is not the thematic point. The fantasy—the headbirth—only intensifies the reality that gave it birth: the number of Germans is relatively small and becoming smaller. In the words of the title, "the Germans are dying out." Whereas the population of the peoples making up the Third World is soaring.

Before proceeding to the story of Harm and Dörte Peters, the teachers from Itzehoe in Holstein, and to the relationship of the story to the demographic theme, one should hark back—following Grass's own sequence—to the population figures in which Grass lumps the two political Germanies, the democratic West and the Communist East (which calls itself, perpetuating a Communist tactical slogan devised in the late 1930s, "democratic"). To the regret of Grass, who has long championed, almost quixotically it would seem, a German reunification, literature is in his opinion the only thing left in the two Germanies that is still held in common. Materialism, whether of the capitalist or Communist sort, blocks any other possibility of their becoming one nation with a single culture.

The overriding marital concern of the Peterses—who, after all, are also a headbirth, an idea on the part of Günter Grass—is whether to have a child: "the child-yes, the child-no," in Grass's succinct and oft-repeated phrase. For it is not a world into which they would insouciantly bring a child. The bases of their reluctance are the well-known ones of wars and threats of wars, nuclear destruction. There are indications that this reluctance, which is not absolute and incessant but relative and periodic, is supplemented at least slightly by their enjoyment of the benefits of self-indulgence and personal flexibility, for example, in their ability to travel to India, Thailand, and Indonesia. Needless to add, those lands offer the possibility of diversion from their concerns about having a child. The latter, however, prove dominant, their effect even heightenend in the environment of the Third World.

Harm and Dörte bear odd names with ironic overtones: the first conveys the same sense in German as in English; the second, a Low German diminutive of Dorothea, evokes also the sense of *dürr* "barren," perhaps also of *dort* "there," alluding to her travel. The travel agency sponsoring the tour that they join is named Sisyphus. As to the relevance of this name we are not restricted to evocation or allusion, for Grass, borrowing admiringly from Camus, makes a point, repeatedly and ironically, of its significance. The agency logo with mythological correctness depicts Sisyphus, the cruel king of Corinth, with the huge stone that he is forever condemned to roll up a steep hill only to have it roll back down again. The brochure explains that Sisyphus Tours are designed for travelers willing to confront hard and disquieting facts in the Third World.

Making preparations for the trip, Dörte is in a child-yes frame of mind and announces that as soon as they have left German nuclear concerns behind, she will throw away her pills. The Peterses arrange to board their cat with a friend in Itzehoe. Harm buys a fine liverwurst, well sealed in plastic, to take to an old school friend whose last address is in Bali. Because the liverwurst episode is based on a similar episode when the Grasses went to China it is not, Grass declares, a headbirth, that is, an idea or a speculation, but a fact. In any event it suggests how closely interwoven in the novel (or filmscript, or simply film) are the Grasses' trip to China and the Peterses' trip to Southeast Asia. The autobiographical trip and the fictional trip reinforce and amplify each other. Grass as the narrator is on both trips, perhaps only slightly less obviously, but still strikingly, on that of the Peterses. As Grass had arrived in China, so the Peterses land in Bombay with two pounds of good German liverwurst in their carryon luggage.

They and a small group from the plane are met by Dr. Konrad Wenthien, Sisyphus's tour leader, a fount of knowledge about Asia, its languages and its cultures. Wenthien's byword is "Asia is different." Decidedly it is, as the traveling teachers are prepared to confirm for themselves under Wenthien's knowing guidance. Whether they land first in

Bombay or in Bangkok, Wenthien is always there (and thus not unlike the narrator). He sees to it that among other things they experience at first hand the gigantic slums of Bombay, or Bangkok, the inhabitants of which buy their water in canisters and the children of which are infested by worms. To the inhabitants of such slums the Peterses' equivocations about having a child are incomprehensible.

Intervening as Günter Grass, the narrator notes that Chinese cities, such as Peking, Shanghai, and Canton, do not have slums. Not until one arrives in Hongkong can one discern the western characteristic of obscene wealth side by side with the grinding poverty of slums. The knowledgeable Dr. Wenthien observes over his regular evening orange juice that it is the East that will determine the future of our planet, that Europe's hunger for the mysteries of Asia will be stilled forever when Europe is overrun by Asia.

From Bombay, or perhaps Bangkok—Grass repeatedly links the Indian city and the Thai city in a speculative entity—the Peterses fly to Bali. In addition to her interest in visiting the slums of Bombay and Bangkok, Dörte has revealed also an interest in figures representing Hindu divinities, for example, Siva, one of the supreme deities in the Hindu pantheon, who among many other things represents the reproductive power. In Bali Dörte's religious interest intensifies into what Harm calls "a religious trip." She discounts reason and performs irrational religious or quasi-religious acts. Joining the native worshipers she implores Siva to bless her with child. Harm becomes impotent.

He meanwhile has been unable to locate his old friend Uwe Jensen, for whom he brought the German liverwurst halfway around the world. Jensen, not to be found at the address that Harm has for him, is reported to have moved on to the island of Timor, perhaps as a smuggler of weapons to East Timor, which is struggling, futilely, to avoid being swallowed by Indonesia. (Although Grass doesn't say so, Indonesia had the advantage of American arms and indulgence.)

Grass observes, not entirely whimsically, that while he was in China he forgot to ask if there were psychoanalysts. His regretful reflection introduces a headbirth, a speculation, of how it would be if Harm and Dörte had gone to a psychoanalyst in Itzehoe. (It becomes more than evident that Grass has a very low opinion of the time-consuming and money-consuming "ritual" of psychoanalysis.) The psychoanalyst might well look like Dr. Wenthien. But Grass is not thinking of a double role. If Wenthien is to have a double role he could also be a guru or a Balinese village priest. But then Grass reverses himself and acknowledges that the same actor could play *all* of the above roles—because all the roles are interchangeable. In that conclusion one clearly recognizes the Grass of *The Flounder*.

Immediately following—surely not by chance—Grass's remarks about psychoanalysis, he dwells on the doubtless even greater peril of an atomic power plant at Brokdorf near Itzehoe. It has not escaped his alarmed attention before, nor that of Harm and Dörte, but not at such bitter length as now. His "film," he declares, must always come back to, and start again from, this atomic power plant, the construction of which has been interrupted for the time being by a lawsuit. For the existence of Dörte's already questionable child depends increasingly on the atomic energy question.

Observing that Orwell's decade is upon the world, that mankind is conditioned to accept every new idiocy as relative progress, Grass—who has already bitterly denounced the alleged neo-fascist policies of the German conservative politician, Franz Josef Strauss—proceeds to the arena of international politics. The new Polish Pope is as infallible as the Ayatollah Khomeini. Though Grass does not name the culprits, as of 1979, it is clear that he is calling Jimmy Carter a bigoted preacher and Leonid Brezhnev a sick philistine, both of whom, keeping the world trembling, may yet deign to announce their decision about what is to happen to the world. Somewhat as Orwell had foreseen, good old capitalism and good old Communism are coming to resemble each other more and more. Grass permits his fantasy to roam: what he would do if he were absolute dictator. Perhaps most adventurously, and quite in consonance with his principle of the interchangeability of roles, he would require the two German states to change their politico-economic system every ten years: in the first decade East Germany could recover by means of capitalism while West Germany was purging itself by means of Communism.

Grass the narrator's flight into fanciful dictatorship is transferred as if by osmosis to his headbirth, Harm Peters, who proclaims war on all the demons and superstitions inhabiting a huge cave in the lava beds near a Balinese volcano. The narrator assures us, however, that he would never permit Harm to misuse his dictatorial powers—by, for example, proscribing the so-called democratic political parties in West Germany. On the other hand, the narrator could well support the abolition of compulsory public taxation for the support of churches, which would compel the church to become as poor as Jesus Christ was.

Inspired by Dörte's admiration of his dictatorial performance, Harm continues in the role. He dictates that the German people in both Germanies voluntarily resolve to die out, and to do so cheerfully, because it will redound to the benefit of humanity. No more procreating (Austrians and Swiss Germans may join in the abstention if they wish). This edict, however, exceeds Dörte's tolerance, for she is now in a child-yes frame of mind. In fact she wants to make love right on the lava, which drives Harm precipitately down the mountainside.

As one probably senses, the travel of the Peterses in Bali becomes increasingly a novelistic means by which the narrator ventilates his opinions, doing so primarily through the mouth of Dr. Wenthien in Bali as well as the pen of Günter Grass in Germany or China. Wenthien predicts that millions of Indians, Egyptians, Mexicans, Javanese, and Chinese will infiltrate Germany. At first the infiltration will be gradual, then in waves, ultimately contaminating the pure blood of the Germanic-Slavic-Celtic hybrid race that now dwells there. The German response will probably be to try to exclude the infiltrators, to build walls. But have walls ever helped? And walls outlive their dubious usefulness. This conclusion leads the narrator as Grass to note the early uselessness of the Great Wall of China, not to speak of the vainness of building the wall in Manila in the sixties to protect the Pope's eye from the view of the awful slums when he visited the dictator Ferdinand Marcos. As if that wall helped anything! The most recent development in wall technology, Grass suggests disgustedly, consists in satellite surveillance, early warning systems, and nuclear wastes.

Harm Peters, declaring that he is not a breeding bull, has had no sexual intercourse with Dörte for all the while that she has been, in his view, "flipped out" religiously. She consults Dr. Wenthien. The narrator tells the reader that he could at this point have Dr. Wenthien recommend that she go on a beach party with the local youths who hang around in front of the resort hotel. But the narrator doesn't wish that; he has no use for the surprises that come from love triangles. Instead Dörte remains true to what she a bit resignedly calls her principles. And tomorrow is departure day. The Peterses still have the German liverwurst, which they may just leave behind or may take back to Germany.

They leave it. But at the last moment it is discovered by a room boy and brought back to the departing teachers. Teachers. . . . Why, Grass ruminates, is he always attracted to pedagogues and pedagogical topics? Reflectively he lists his works or characters in the pedagogical rubric: *Cat and Mouse;* and the teacher, Miss Spollenhauer, in *The Tin Drum,* trying to teach Oskar; the teacher Brunies, with his craving for candy, in *Dog Years*; the teacher Starusch, with his toothaches, in *Local Anaesthetic;* in *From the Diary of a Snail,* Hermann Ott, Doubt, confined in Stomma's basement for the duration of the war, remains a teacher; and even the Flounder proves his mettle as a pedagogue. Maybe, Grass suggests, his own abiding interest in teachers and teaching is owing to the fact that his growing children bring school home with them every day.

The Grasses left China and flew back to Germany in fall 1979. The Peterses return at the end of August 1980. Because that date is projected in advance of the date at which the narrator writes (fall and early winter 1979), then, according to the narrator, they must already know the outcome of the lawsuit aiming to block the construction of the Brokdorf nuclear plant, supported by—naturally—the sponsoring corporations as well as the state of Schleswig-Holstein. The narrator doesn't know the outcome himself yet. But he does know that West Germany is irrevocably geared to growth, to material progress, that the essential German characteristic is to make the impossible possible. Further, to do it fast. He has evidently erred in setting store by the snail.

Back home, when they go to pick up their cat, the Peterses discover that it—she—has five three-day-old kittens. Harm and Dörte, surrogate parents of a sort, resume their school careers, prepared to put their recent trip to pedagogical use. A student inquires of Dörte if she is at last pregnant. We know that the answer is no. Furthermore, she is about to enter a child-no frame of mind again, while her husband, advocating child-yes, throws her pills down the toilet. At this significant but doubtless indefinitive point the narrator notes that the film must end, while school and politics continue. The Russians invade Afghanistan, the idiocy spreads. Grass's summations are not far from apocalyptic, a perspective that the reader may conclude is not entirely dependent on his fondness for seventeenth-century German poetry, although the latter may have served to reinforce the gloomy picture, the film, of the contemporary world that he presents in *Headbirths*.

Critics of traditional persuasion may urge that the half-fictional embodiment of very recent experience amounts to something like a newsletter *from* the writer rather than a book *by* the writer. In this case, one might be tempted to add—the form is more than hospitable to asides—Grass anticipates an important facet of such recrimination, the charge that he lacks the necessary distance from the events narrated. He cheerfully acknowledges that such criticism is correct. It is true: in school he and his classmates learned that after the past (Vergangenheit) comes the present (Gegenwart), which is followed by the future (Zukunft). But because he deals with yet a fourth variety of time—which we have called simultaneity—he is not obliged to maintain the purity of form and sequence that might be enhanced by distancing. This fourth variety of time, embodying portions of all three German time words, he calls *Vergegenkunft*.

The cleverness and even more the validity of this retort to one side, it may be suggested that the fictional characters in *Headbirths,* such as Harm and Dörte Peters, tend not to be characters of much interest or complexity. Even Dr. Wenthien seems superficial. To be sure, Grass makes no secret of his manipulation of the characters, takes the reader into his workshop. That is rewarding, but the price is characters whom one sees too clearly as puppets, as types. To some extent the conceit that the book is a film compensates for the dilution of the character complexity that can be achieved on paper. Looked at another way, the filmic conception itself contributes to the poverty of character. But finally and ironically, if roles, like times, are readily interchangeable, as the reader is persuaded within the novel, one should scarcely lament the absence of depth or complexity of character. On the other hand, *Headbirths* represents Grass's boldest step yet in innovative fictional structure. Or at the very least, because of the filmic conciseness of the novel, the alternation between Grass the fictive narrator and Grass the autobiographer and politically engaged author strikes us with particular force.

# Conclusions

Grass is a magnificent writer in the literal sense of the adjective: he does great things. Great, first and most obviously, as to versatility: poetry, drama, essays, novella, novels of increasingly innovative cast. Not to forget his versatility in other realms of art—that is, music, sculpture, and drawing, of which the last, in the form of book-jacket designs, is most evidently and integrally related to his writing. While it is undoubtedly Grass's novels, plus the one drama, *The Plebeians Rehearse the Uprising,* that have won him his extensive English-language readership, those readers will deepen their understanding and appreciation of Grass by gaining at least some familiarity with his essays, his speeches, his poetry, and even his less-well-known plays. As he says, dialogue is basic, and it is by no means confined to his novels. It is the compelling underlying form for the emergence of images—perhaps essentially artistic images—on the printed page.

Grass is a great innovator. The relationship of his early plays to the drama of the absurd is problematic. Certainly he was not well acquainted with the French absurdist drama when he undertook his own lyric-derived, dialogue-based, action-poor experimental plays. It is in the novel, however, that Grass's innovativeness has found its greatest scope. While the structure of *The Tin Drum* still contains earmarks of the linear novel of the nineteenth century, his recent novels make increasing use of simultaneity as well as equilocation. Not ornamentally or just cleverly, but thematically. Believing as he does that fiction is truer than

153

history, he magisterially rearranges historical details in the
service of his fiction. In such blended fiction it is natural that
Günter Grass should appear not only in the personae of a
variety of simultaneous fictional (perhaps basically historical)
narrators, but also, quite overtly, as Günter Grass himself,
writer, father, husband, political activist, German—and a
German whose purview ranges from Danzig to the entire
world.

The great expectations aroused by *The Tin Drum* in 1959
have hardly been disappointed in his subsequent fiction. One
might observe that *The Tin Drum* was a difficult feat to
follow, and yet Grass has been doing just that with little
letdown in the decades since the appearance of that first
novel. Not by continually replicating *The Tin Drum*, as some
imperceptive critics suggested was the case with the rest of
The Danzig Trilogy. Their implication was that once Grass
had written himself out of his Danzig youth, he would prove
to have little more to say. In the first place, such a critical
view reflects a one-dimensional reading of *The Tin Drum*,
which is distinctly a multidimensional work. In the second
place, Grass has had abundantly more to say, whether the
Danzig connection is in the foreground or whether it is
allowed to recede into the background.

It is quite true that his Danzig characters reappear under
different (although not necessarily unrelated) circumstances
in subsequent works, both of the trilogy and after the trilogy.
The most noteworthy reemergence may be that of the former
youth-gang leader Störtebeker in his later appearance as a
troubled—dentally and otherwise—high-school teacher
whose students are quite uninterested in his youthful derring-
do. But Grass's ultimate fictional universe has proved
anything but parochial; rather it embraces an almost
spectacular range of geography and epoch. And since The
Danzig Trilogy, as an unremittingly committed writer, he has
indeed had more to say (even more about Danzig). That this is
true is largely owing to that very commitment, to the
seriousness with which he takes his role as an engaged writer.

One gets the clue from the fact that he regards the term, engaged writer, as a tautology. One sees the clue confirmed in the string of novels as well as in *The Plebeians Rehearse the Uprising* and *Max: A Play,* which draw on his social and political commitment. Once again his antagonists were confounded, this time in the assumption that no one could successfully combine the careers of man of letters and political activist—virtually politician—and that letters would be the loser. To the contrary, letters have gained.

Grass's breaking the taboo—predominantly German but to an extent contemporarily American as well—against a writer's involving himself in the issues of the day was an act of conviction and courage. Politicians (or their speechwriters) write all too plentifully. But here is a writer who not only joins the political fray in other than a merely decorative fashion, but is willing to do so in a grinding, footslogging, every-day-another-hotel-room campaign. As to the reason for his year in, year out, conspicuous as well as inconspicuous political engagement: perhaps few writers have had quite so much reason as Grass to be so fearful of a revival of Nazism. For not only was he exposed to Nazism during his formative years; but also, by his own account, he did not question it at the time. (One has to admit that his worst fears of a rebirth of Nazism have not been realized; one may pray for a similar misgauging of the fate of the consumer society as well as of the perils associated with nuclear energy.)

Grass's commitment is accompanied by a devastating irony, from which he does not exempt himself—if, as appears to be the case, he is the fictive narrator as well as Günter Grass, both of whom continue to inhabit his novels. The irony is the means by which he is able to confront the failure of man's—and woman's—institutions, above all in the present century, but in the present century as the heir of past centuries. For his female characters and institutions show every sign of the historic fallibility of their male counterparts. Matriarchy, both ancient and prospective, as in *The Flounder,* is the prime case in point, a case for which Grass, rendered even more vulnerable by what some may see as obscenity, has received severe criticism from feminists. But he is only saying: don't be like men; maybe there is a different, a better way. None of us, of whichever sex and whatever nationality, can afford to continue behaving the way we have in the past.

# Notes

## 1. The Plays

1. Marianne Kesting, *Panorama des zeitgenössischen Theaters* (Munich: Piper, 1969), p. 302.
2. The speech may well have contributed to the earlier, more anti-Brecht interpretation of the play. See Ann L. Mason, *The Skeptical Muse: A Study of Günter Grass's Conception of the Artist* (Bern: Herbert Lang, 1974), p. 98.

## 2. The Tin Drum

1. Interview with Geno Hartlaub, *Sonntagsblatt,* Hamburg, January 1, 1967.
2. John Toland, *Adolf Hitler* (New York: Doubleday, 1976), p. 212.
3. For an extended mythic interpretation see Edward Diller, *A Mythic Journey: Günter Grass's "Tin Drum"* (Lexington, Kentucky: The University Press of Kentucky, 1974).
4. An excellent detailed analysis, in English, of *The Tin Drum* is to be found in John Reddick, *The "Danzig Trilogy" of Günter Grass* (New York: Harcourt Brace Jovanovich, 1975), from which I have drawn in my discussion of *The Tin Drum.*

## 3. Cat and Mouse

1. Walter Höllerer in an interview with John Reddick,

157

January 1966. Cited by Reddick, *The "Danzig Trilogy"
of Günter Grass* (New York: Harcourt Brace Jovanovich,
1975), p. 89.

2. See Karl H. Ruhleder, "A Pattern of Messianic Thought
   in Günter Grass' *Katz und Maus,*" *German Quarterly*
   39 (1966): 599-612.

## 4. Dog Years

1. As Grass himself declared, "The last novel of these three
   books that have to do with Danzig, *Dog Years* is also
   the most political." From an interview (1971) with
   Gertrude Cepl-Kaufmann, *Günter Grass. Eine Analyse
   des Gesamtwerkes unter dem Aspekt von Literatur und
   Politik* (Kronberg/Taunus.: Scriptor, 1975), p. 295.

2. Günter Grass, *Dokumente zur politischen Wirkung,* ed.
   Heinz Ludwig Arnold and Franz Josef Görtz (Munich:
   Text + Kritik, 1971), editorial foreword, p. viii.

3. Cited in *Dokumente zur politischen Wirkung,* pp. viii-
   ix. See also p. 1.

## 6. Local Anaesthetic/Max: A Play

1. The otherwise helpful article in *Time* Magazine, April
   13, 1970, pp. 68-79, declares: "Grass is Starusch,
   essentially." But Grass is not Starusch only. Excessively
   concerned to work Grass into an American framework,
   the article also goes overboard in making him a hero of
   the middle class.

2. For at least one critic, "Scherbaum's conversion remains
   unexplained." See Irène Leonard, *Günter Grass* (New
   York: Barnes and Noble, 1974), p. 69. The perceived
   inexplicablity derives from Leonard's wish to magnify
   the dentist's autonomy vis-à-vis Starusch and Scherbaum.

## 9. The Flounder

1. Interview with Fritz Raddartz in *Die Zeit,* August 12,
   1977. An excellent book-length study, in English, of
   *The Flounder* is the collection of essays entitled *"The*

*Fisherman and His Wife": Günter Grass's "The Flounder" in Critical Perspective,* ed. Siegfried Mews (New York: AMS Press, 1983).

2. Heinz Ludwig Arnold, "Gespräche mit Günter Grass," *Text + Kritik* 1/1a, 5th ed. (1978): pp. 1-39; see esp. p. 31.

## 10. The Meeting at Telgte

1. Georg Rudolf Weckherlin (1584-1653), one of the most important poets of the early baroque period, tried to write a genuine German poetry after French models, went to England in 1620, where he became a close associate of Milton. Johann Michael Moscherosch (1601-1669), best known for *The Visions of Philander von Sittewald,* a scathing satire on morality in Germany during the Thirty Years' War. Johann Matthian Schneuber (1614-1665), professor and editor of poetry, helped found the Strasbourg literature and language society, The Upright Fir Tree Society, later a member of the more durable Fruit-Gathering Society in Anhalt (Schneuber is surely one of the more obscure participants in the Telgte meeting). Daniel Czepko von Reigersfeld (1605-1660), mystic poet. Friedrich von Logau (1604-1655), famed for his epigrams. Christian Hoffmann von Hoffmannswaldau (1617-1679), writer of bombastic poetry. Johann Scheffler (1624-1677), later known as Angelus Silesius, a leading mystic poet. Johann Rist (1607-1676), poet, dramatist, founder of the Hamburg literature and language society, The Order of the Elbe River Swans. Paul Gerhardt (1607-1676), writer of hymn lyrics. Simon Dach (1605-1659), bourgeois poet with mystic leanings. Georg Philipp Harsdörffer (1607-1658), writer of religious and pastoral poetry, founder of the literature and language society in Nuremburg. Sigmund von Birken (1626-1681), pastoral poet, influential in the literature and language society in Nuremburg.

# Bibliography

## I. Principal Books by Günter Grass in German

The following is a relatively complete listing of books, however short they may be. It does not, however, claim to list every book of ten or twelve pages. Frequently material comprising a book on first publication has been incorporated into a subsequent collection in a single larger book. (In the unique case of *Beritten hin und zurück* the original periodical publication is listed.) The accessibility of a given form of publication in the United States and Canada is a factor in listing here, so that sometimes relatively inaccessible first publications may be omitted in favor of generally accessible collections containing the work in question. Grass in addition has published hundreds of essays in magazines and newspapers. For them, at least until 1977, and for data on original (and sometimes partial) publication of book items through that year, the reader is referred to the extensive bibliographies of Everett, Görtz, O'Neill, and Woods, listed under III below, as well as the bibliography sections of Cepl-Kaufmann and Neuhaus, listed under IV below.

## A. Poetry

*Die Vorzüge der Windhühner.* Neuwied: Luchterhand, 1956.
*Gleisdreieck.* Neuwied: Luchterhand, 1960.

*Ausgefragt.* Neuwied: Luchterhand, 1967.

*Gesammelte Gedichte.* Neuwied: Luchterhand, 1971.

*Mariazuehren. Hommageàmarie. Inmarypraise.* Photos by Maria Rama. Munich: Bruckmann, 1973.

*Liebe geprüft.* Bremen: Carl Schünemann, 1974.

## B. Plays

*Noch zehn Minuten bis Buffalo.* Berlin: Kiepenheuer, 1957.

"Beritten hin und zurück. Ein Vorspiel auf dem Theater." *Akzente,* No. 5, 1958, pp. 399-409.

*Die bösen Köche.* Berlin: Kiepenheuer, 1961.

*Hochwasser.* Frankfurt am Main: Suhrkamp, 1963.

*Onkel, Onkel.* Berlin: Klaus Wagenbach, 1965.

*Die Plebejer proben den Aufstand.* Neuwied: Luchterhand, 1966.

*Davor.* Berlin: Kiepenheuer, 1969.

*Theaterspiele.* Neuwied: Luchterhand, 1970. (Contains: *Hochwasser; Onkel, Onkel; Nochzehn Minuten bis Buffalo: Die bösen Köche; Die Plebejer proben den Aufstand; Davor.)*

## C. Fiction

*Die Blechtrommel.* Neuwied: Luchterhand, 1959.

*Katz und Maus.* Neuwied: Luchterhand, 1961.

*Hundejahre.* Neuwied: Luchterhand, 1963.

*örtlich betäubt.* Neuwied: Luchterhand, 1969.

*Aus dem Tagebuch einer Schnecke.* Neuwied: Luchterhand, 1972.

*Der Butt.* Neuwied: Luchterhand, 1977.

*Das Treffen in Telgte.* Neuwied: Luchterhand, 1979.

*Kopfgeburten oder Die Deutschen sterben aus.* Neuwied: Luchterhand, 1980.

## D. Political Writings

*Dich singe ich Demokratie.* Neuwied: Luchterhand, 1965.

*Des Kaisers neue Kleider.* Neuwied: Luchterhand, 1965.

*Ich klage an!* Neuwied: Luchterhand, 1965.

*Der Fall Axel C. Springer am Beispiel Arnold Zweig.*
Berlin: Voltaire, 1967.

*Briefe über die Grenze. Versuch eines Ost-West Dialogs*
(with Pavel Kohout). Hamburg: Christian Wegner,
1968.

*Über das Selbstverständliche. Politische Schriften.* Neuwied:
Luchterhand, 1968.

*Dokumente zur politischen Wirkung.* Ed. Heinz Ludwig
Arnold and Franz Josef Görtz. Stuttgart: Boorberg,
1971.

*Der Bürger und seine Stimme. Reden, Aufsätze,
Kommentare.* Neuwied: Luchterhand, 1974.

*Denkzettel. Politische Reden und Aufsätze 1965-1976.*
Neuwied: Luchterhand, 1978.

## E. Literary Criticism

*Über meinen Lehrer Döblin und andere Vorträge.* Berlin:
Literarisches Colloquium, 1968.
*Aufsätze zur Literatur.* Neuwied: Luchterhand, 1980.

## F. Dancing and Film

*Die Ballerina.* Berlin: Friedenauer Presse, 1963.
*Die Blechtrommel als Film* (with Volker Schlöndorff).
Frankfurt am Main: Zweitausendundeins, 1979.

## G. Drawings (with Texts)

*Zeichnungen und Texte* 1954-1977. Ed. Anselm Dreher.
Text Selection and Afterword by Sigrid Mayer.
Neuwied: Luchterhand, 1982.

## II. Works by Günter Grass in English

## A. Poetry

*Selected Poems.* Tr. Michael Hamburger and Christopher
Middleton. New York: Harcourt, Brace and World,

1966. (Contains selected poems from *Vorzüge der Windhüner* and *Gleisdreieck*.)

*New Poems*. Tr. Michael Hamburger. New York: Harcourt, Brace and World, 1968. (Contains selected poems from *Ausgefragt*.)

*Poems of Günter Grass*. Tr. Michael Hamburger and Christopher Middleton. Intro. Michael Hamburger. Harmondsworth: Penguin, 1969. (A combined edition of *Selected Poems* and *New Poems*.)

*Inmarypraise*. Tr. Christopher Middleton. Photos by Maria Rama. New York: Harcourt Brace Jovanovich, 1974.

*Love Tested*. Tr. Michael Hamburger. New York: Harcourt Brace Jovanovich, 1975. (Limited edition of 25 copies.)

*In the Egg and Other Poems*. Tr. Michael Hamburger and Christopher Middleton. New York: Harcourt Brace Jovanovich, 1977. (Similar to *Poems of Günter Grass,* above, but without the introduction.)

## B. Plays

*Four Plays*. Tr. Ralph Manheim and A. Leslie Willson. Intro. Martin Esslin. New York: Harcourt, Brace and World, 1967. (Contains: *Flood; Mister, Mister; Only Ten Minutes to Buffalo,* tr. Ralph Manheim; *The Wicked Cooks,* tr. A. Leslie Willson.)

*The Plebeians Rehearse the Uprising*. Tr. Ralph Manheim. New York: Harcourt, Brace and World, 1967.

*Rocking Back and Forth*. Tr. Michael Benedikt and Joseph Goradza. In *Postwar German Theatre*. Ed. and tr. Michael Benedikt and George E. Wellwarth. New York: Dutton, 1967, pp. 261-75.

*Max: A Play*. Tr. A. Leslie Willson and Ralph Manheim. New York: Harcourt Brace Jovanovich, 1972.

## C. Fiction

*The Tin Drum*. Tr. Ralph Manheim. New York: Pantheon, 1962.

*Cat and Mouse.* Tr. Ralph Manheim. New York: Harcourt, Brace and World, 1963.

*Dog Years.* Tr. Ralph Manheim. New York: Harcourt, Brace and World, 1965.

*Local Anaesthetic.* Tr. Ralph Manheim. New York: Harcourt, Brace and World, 1968.

*From the Diary of a Snail.* Tr. Ralph Manheim. New York: Harcourt Brace Jovanovich, 1973.

*The Flounder.* Tr. Ralph Manheim. New York: Harcourt Brace Jovanovich, 1978.

*The Meeting at Telgte.* Tr. Ralph Manheim. New York: Harcourt Brace Jovanovich, 1981.

*Headbirths or The Germans Are Dying Out.* Tr. Ralph Manheim. New York: Harcourt Brace Jovanovich, 1982.

## D.  Political Writings

*Speak Out! Speeches, Open Letters, Commentaries.* Tr. Ralph Manheim and others. Intro. Michael Harrington. New York: Harcourt, Brace and World, 1969.

## III.  Bibliographies of Günter Grass

Everett, George A. *A Select Bibliography of Günter Grass* (From 1956 to 1973). New York: Burt Franklin, 1974.

Görtz, Franz Josef. "Kommentierte Auswahl-Bibliographie." *Text + Kritik,* Nos. 1/1a, 5th series, June 1978, pp. 175-99.

O'Neill, Patrick. *Günter Grass: A Bibliography 1955-1975.* Toronto: University of Toronto Press, 1976.

Woods, Jean M. "Günter Grass Bibliography." *West Coast Review* 5, No. 3, 1971, pp. 52-56; and 6, No. 1, 1971, pp. 31-40.

# IV. Selected Works about Günter Grass

## A. Books

Arnold, Heinz Ludwig, ed. *Text + Kritik,* Nos. 1/ 1a, "Über Günter Grass." Aachen: Georgi, [1965].

————, ed. *Text + Kritik,* Nos. 1/ 1a, 5th ed., "Günter Grass." Munich: Edition Text + Kritik, 1978.

Brode, Hanspeter. *Günter Grass.* Munich: Beck, 1979.

Cepl-Kaufmann, Gertrude. *Günter Grass. Eine Analyse des Gesamtwerkes unter dem Aspekt von Literatur und Politik.* Kronberg Taunus.: Scriptor, 1975.

Cunliffe, W. Gordon. *Günter Grass.* New York: Twayne, 1969.

Diller, Edward. *A Mythic Journey: Günter Grass's "Tin Drum."* Lexington, Kentucky: The University Press of Kentucky, 1974.

GeiRler, Rolf, ed. *Günter Grass. Ein Materialienbuch.* Neuwied: Luchterhand, 1976.

Gerstenberg, Renate E.. *Zur Erzähltechnik von Günter Grass.* Heidelberg: Winter, 1980.

Görtz, Franz Josef. *Günter Grass. Zur Pathogense eines Markenbilds.* Meisenheim am Glan: Hain, 1978.

Hollington, Michael. *Günter Grass: The Writer in a Pluralist Society.* London: Marion Boyars, 1980.

Jendrowiak, Silke. *Günter Grass und die "Hybris" des Kleinbürgers.* Heidelberg: Winter, 1979.

Jurgensen, Manfred, ed. *Grass. Kritik — Thesen — Analysen.* Bern: Francke, 1973.

————. *Über Günter Grass. Untersuchungen zur sprachbildlichen Rollenfunktion.* Bern: Francke, 1974.

Leonard, Irène. *Günter Grass.* New York: Barnes and Noble, 1974.

Mason, Ann L. *The Skeptical Muse: A Study of Günter Grass' Conception of the Artist.* Bern: Herbert Lang, 1974.

Mews, Siegfried, ed. *"The Fisherman and His Wife":*

*Günter Grass's "The Flounder"in Critical Perspective.*
New York: AMS Press, 1983.

Miles, Keith. *Günter Grass.* New York: Barnes and Noble, 1975.

Neuhaus, Volker. *Günter Grass.* Stuttgart: Metzler, 1979.

Pickar, Gertrud Bauer, ed. *Adventures of a Flounder: Critical essays on Günter Grass'"Der Butt."* Munich: Fink, 1982.

Reddick, John. *The "Danzig Trilogy" of Günter Grass.* New York: Harcourt Brace Jovanovich, 1975.

Richter, Frank-Raymund. *Günter Grass. Die Verganheitsbewältigung in der Danziger Trilogie.* Bonn: Bouvier, 1979.

Rölleke, Heinz. *Der wahre Butt.* Düsseldorf: Diederichs, 1978.

Rothenberg, Jürgen. *Günter Grass—Das Chaos in verbesserter Ausführung.* Heidelberg: Winter, 1976.

Schlöndorff, Volker. *"Die Blechtrommel." Tagebuch einer Verfilmung.* Neuwied: Luchterhand, 1979.

Schwarz, Wilhelm J. *Der Erzähler Günter Grass.* Bern: Francke, 1969; 2nd enlarged ed., 1971.

White, Ray Lewis. *Günter Grass in America: The Early Years.* Hildesheim and New York: Olms, 1981.

Willson, A. Leslie, ed. *A Günter Grass Symposium.* Austin: University of Texas Press, 1971.

## B. Articles and chapters

Abbott, Scott H. "Günter Grass' *Hundejahre:* A Realistic Novel about Myth." *German Quarterly* 55 (1982): 212-20.

Arnold, Heinz Ludwig. "Kleine Anmerkung zu Günter Grass: Über den Zusammenhang seiner Prosawerke der 70er Jahre." *Modern Languages* 63 (1982): 181-83.

Beyersdorf, H.E. "The Narrator as Artful Deceiver: Aspects of Narrative Perspective in *Die Blechtrommel."* *Germanic Review* 55 (1980): 129-38.

Blomster, Wesley V. "The Documentation of a Novel: Otto Weininger and *Hundejahre* by Günter Grass." *Monatshefte* 61 (1969): 122-38.

Butler, G.P. "Übersetzt klingt alles plausibel': Some Notes on *Der Butt* and *The Flounder.*" *German Life and Letters* 34 (1980-81): 3-10.

Caltvedt, Lester. "Oskar's Account of Himself: Narrative 'Guilt' and the Relationship of Fiction to History in *Die Blechtrommel.*" *Seminar* 14 (1978): 284-94.

Campbell, Anne. "The Grotesque as a Critical Concept: A Question of Cultural Values." *Seminar* 15 (1979): 251-61.

Cory, Mark E. "Sisyphus and the Snail: Metaphors for the Political Process in Günter Grass' *Aus dem Tagebuch einer Schnecke* and *Kopfgeburten oder Die Deutschen sterben aus.*" *German Studies Review* 6 (1983): 519-33.

Durzak, Manfred. "Günter Grass." In Karl H. Van D'Elden, ed., *West German Poets on Society and Politics.* Detroit: Wayne State University Press, 1979, pp. 162-79.

————. "Plädoyer für eine Rezeptionsästhetik. Anmerkungen zur deutschen und amerikanischen Literaturkritik am Beispiel von Günter Grass, *örtlich betäubt.*" *Akzente* 18 (1971): 487-504.

Friedrichsmeyer, Erhard M. "Aspects of Myth, Parody and Obscenity in Grass' *Die Blechtrommel* and *Katz und Maus.*" *Germanic Review* 40 (1965): 240-50.

Hamburger, Michael. "Moralist and Jester: The Poetry of Günter Grass." In *Art as Second Nature.* Cheadle: Carcanet New Press, 1975, pp. 134-49.

Hatfield, Henry. "Günter Grass: The Artist as Satirist." In Robert R. Heitner, ed., *The Contemporary Novel in German: A Symposium.* Austin: University of Texas Press, 1967, pp. 115-34.

Hoffmeister, Werner. "Dach, Distel und die Dichter. Günter Grass' *Das Treffen in Telgte.*" *Zeitschrift für deutsche Philologie* 100 (1981): 274-87.

Koopmann, Helmut. "Günter Grass. Der Faschismus als Kleinbürgertum und was daraus wurde." In Hans Wagener, ed., *Gegenwartsliteratur und Drittes Reich.* Stuttgart: Reclam, 1977, pp. 163-82.

Mews, Siegfried. "Grass' *Kopfgeburten:* The Writer in Orwell's Decade." *German Studies Review* 6 (1983): 501-17.

Mouton, Janice. "Gnomes, Fairy-Tale Heroes, and Oskar Matzerath." *Germanic Review* 56 (1981): 28-33.

Pickar, Gertrud Bauer. "Intentional Ambiguity in Günter Grass' *Katz und Maus.*" *Orbis Litterarum* 26 (1971): 233-45.

——— "*Silberpappeln* and *Saatkartoffeln:* The Interaction of Art and Reality in Grass' *Die Plebejer proben den Aufstand.*" In Edward R. Haymes, ed., *Theatrum Mundi: Essays on German Drama and German Literature.* Munich: Fink, 1980, pp. 198-220.

Reddick, John. "Action and Impotence: Günter Grass's *örtlich betaübt.*" *Modern Language Review* 67 (1972): 563-78.

Roberts, David. "The Cult of the Hero: An Interpretation of *Katz und Maus.*" *German Life and Letters* 29 (1975-76): 307-22.

Rohlfs, J. W. "Chaos or Order? Günter Grass's *Kopfgeburten.*" *Modern Language Review* 77 (1982): 886-93.

Ruhleder, Karl H. "A Pattern of Messianic Thought in Günter Grass' *Katz und Maus.*" *German Quarterly* 39 (1966): 599-612.

Russell, Peter. "Floundering on Feminism: The Meaning of Günter Grass's *Der Butt.*" *German Life and Letters* 33 (1979-80): 245-56.

Schade, Richard Erich. "Poet and Artist: Iconography in Grass' *Treffen in Telgte.*" *German Quarterly* 55 (1982): 200-211.

Slaymaker, William. "Who cooks, Winds Up: The Dilemma of Freedom in Grass? *Die Blechtrommel* and

*Hundejahre.*" *Colloquia Germanica* 14 (1981): 48-68.

Stowell, H. Peter. "Grass's *Dog Years:* Apocalypse, the Old and the New." *Perspectives on Contemporary Literature* 5 (1979): 79-96.

Verweyen, Theodor and Gunther Witting. "Polyhistors neues Glück. Zu Günter Grass; Erzählung *Das Treffen in Telgte* und ihrer Kritik." *Germanisch-Romanische Monatsschrift* 30 (1980): 451-65.

Williams, Gerhild S. "Es war einmal, ist und wird wieder sein: Geschichte und Geschichten in Günter Grass, *Der Butt.*" In Paul Michael Lützeler, und Egon Schwarz, eds. *Deutsche Literatur in der Bundesrepublik seit 1965: Untersuchungen und Berichte. Königstein/Taunus:* Athenäum, 1980, pp. 182-94.

# Index

171